The Hitler Scoop

Revel Barker

First published in Great Britain by
Pen Press Publishers Ltd
39–41, North Road
Islington
London N7 9DP

ISBN 1 904754 30 9

Revel Barker started writing for newspapers while still at school and joined the *Yorkshire Evening Post* in Leeds before becoming the youngest reporter ever employed by the *Daily Mirror*.

As a reporter, defence correspondent, foreign editor, and managing editor he travelled the world, gaining first hand experience of many of the situations and meeting many of the people described in *The Hitler Scoop*.

He now lives on an island in the Mediterranean.

Also by Revel Barker

Non-fiction:

Round Up The Usual Suspects (editor)

Field Of Vision

'Journalism is the only form of human activity where the orgasm comes at the beginning' – Vincent Mulchrone, chief feature writer of the *Daily Mail*, to the author, 1966

'Journalists are always very interested – in what they are doing' – Neil Armstrong, astronaut, to the author, 1996

Author's Note

I am indebted, for assistance during the writing of this book, to: the late Lord Dacre (formerly Hugh Trevor-Roper, author of *The Last Days Of Hitler*), who interviewed Dr Theo Morell in 1945 and kindly told me of his experience; to German journalist Otmar Katz, who interviewed Mrs Morell in Munich in June 1967 and edited her late husband's medical diaries; Dr Frank Whitford of Wolfson College, Cambridge; Dr Jonathan Secker Walker formerly of University College Hospital, London; Tom Rhodes, of *The European* and later of *The Times*; Ted Levite in Tel Aviv; V J Eastes, librarian of E Merck Ltd (established in the UK in 1970); and to Robert Wolfe and Paul Rood of the Captured Records Staff at the National Archives and Records Administration, Washington DC, for access to Dr Morell's personal diaries.

Any factual and historical errors and inaccuracies are mine alone; I say that, although it shouldn't make any difference in a novel, but much of the background in this story is true. Certainly, where prominent people appear, they are in the main in their correct historical context, and their quotes are generally genuine quotes.

The exceptions are Dr and Mrs Morell. History records that Dr Morell, cleared of war crimes with certificate number 52160 on June 20, 1947, died of arteriosclerosis with damage to the myocardial muscles in May 1948, in the Alpenhof district hospital, Tegernsee, aged 61.

His widow Johanna (Hanni) died in Munich in 1967.

ONE

Spring, 1967

Within twenty-four hours of crossing the Irish Sea, Charles Ritter had been hit by an obvious fact: if you're a German farmer and the IRA has bombed and burned your home and outbuildings, the odds are against your being around for an interview with a passing Fleet Street hack.

According to the police in Dublin, five foreign-owned farms in the Irish Republic, which had all been mysteriously set ablaze over the weekend, had been the subjects of a concerted IRA campaign. Ritter had already driven to four of them, without meeting a farmer. And not only were the foreign farmers not available: the neighbours in the villages were no help, either. Now, in the fifth village, Ritter wandered unconfidently into a grocer's shop, which clearly doubled as a bar.

'Good morning. Forty, no, sixty, Rothmans, please. I wonder... do you know where I might find Doctor Falk?'

'Who?' The shopkeeper made it sound as if he'd never heard the name.

'Doctor Falk; the German who farms the land behind this store.'

'Is he not at the farm, then?'

'It burned down on Saturday.'

'Well I never! The things you learn from visitors!'

Given that the store was at the end of the farm drive, that there was an uninterrupted view of the charred remains from the store's front doorstep, and that the weekend's blaze must have lighted the sky for miles around, Ritter thought he should try another tack.

'Is it too early for a drink?'

'It's never too early for me.'

'Then I'll have a large CDG with tonic, please, plus whatever you'd like yourself.'

The grocer, unimpressed by his English customer's display of local drinking knowledge, reached for a bottle, unscrewed the cap and guessed a generous double measure of Cork Dry Gin, then put a bottle of Canadian Club tonic beside it and sucked in his cheeks, thoughtfully.

'I think I'll have a cup of tea.'

He mainly stayed in his back room while the kettle boiled, reappearing briefly twice in answer to the lifting of the shop door sneck and the tinkling of a bell on a coiled spring, to serve customers. Ritter watched as the shopkeeper carved exactly half a pound of butter from a cylinder half the size of a barrel and then patted it into the shape of a pre-packed block; for another customer he estimated, with a metal scoop drawing from a bin, one pound of sugar, which he poured into a stiff blue paper bag. He tossed it onto the scales: it had been an exact estimate. The grocer folded the bag so that the sugar was sealed securely. Ritter remembered that they used to do something similar at his local Co-op, but not as accurately, and he hadn't seen it done for years.

When he came back to the linoleum-covered counter with a teapot, milk jug, sugar bowl and two cups and saucers, the grocer studied Ritter in silence for a few minutes.

'Is it business you'll be after having with your man, then?'

'According to the *Gardai*, his farm was burned down by the IRA. It's clearly been burned down by somebody. I wanted to talk to him about that.'

'But you're not from the *Gardai*, surely?'

'I'm from London. I'm a reporter on the *Post*. I wanted to talk to him about why his farm was burned down.'

'And you expect him to know the answer to that, do you?'

'Who would, if he doesn't?'

'Well, I'm no reporter and I have no training and little education to speak of, unlike yourself for example. But I would have thought the boys to ask would be the boys who burned it down.'

Ritter's face brightened. 'And do you know them?'

'Now, I wouldn't rightly know them at all. Nor even if the people you'd think you're lookin' for were the people you should be lookin' for. The people who'll know that will be the *Gardai*, and they're in Dublin, I expect. They must know them – otherwise they could not in honesty say who it was did it, now, could they?'

Ritter pretended to appreciate the logic of the argument. He thanked the shopkeeper for his service, paid for the drinks and went outside to a telephone kiosk to phone his office. There were, he reported, no German farmers at any of the five farms bombed during the previous weekend. The story, if any, had to be with the IRA and with the *Gardai* at police headquarters, and that meant returning to Dublin with the hope of some cooperation from the *Post*'s Dublin office. It was still Monday morning; his copy was wanted for Wednesday morning's paper, which meant filing by the time the news desk came back from lunch on Tuesday, some time after three. Wednesday's *Post* was going to be the start of an Irish circulation drive. Monica, the news desk secretary, said she would book him in, overnight, at the Gresham.

The sun was high and the day hot and getting hotter. Ritter was aware of the Dry Gin filling his head. He should have asked for only a single. Better, he should have been as wise as the grocer and settled for a cup of tea. The grocer had even provided an extra cup, obviously in expectation of exactly that thought occurring to his customer. He hoped that it was nothing more serious than the gin that he could feel behind his eyebrows, and still smell, inside the bridge of his nose.

By noon he realised that although it might have been the gin that triggered the sensation it wasn't the alcohol that was now pressing behind his right eye. He lowered both offside windows in his Sunbeam Rapier – the rally car was designed so that the central side column wound down with the rear passenger window, leaving a complete open space from front quarter-light to rear corner of the car.

The windstream rustled piles of yellowing newspapers and empty cigarette packets around on the back seat. He adjusted the quarter-light so that the cooling air was directed on to his right temple as his tyres crunched over the shale chippings through the country lanes. It was, he realised, to no avail. He was going down with the first in a series of migraine attacks.

According to a pamphlet they'd given him in Charterhouse Square, migraine was 'the cruellest pain known to mankind'. Some women friends had argued with Ritter that it couldn't possibly be worse than childbirth, and Ritter had countered that that was probably why the Migraine Centre had said mankind, not womankind – but that if the pain of childbirth was in fact worse than migraine, there would be no brothers or sisters in the civilised world. His mother would have known. She'd suffered from migraine – they said it was hereditary, transmitted from mother to son (but in that case how did mothers get it, in the first place?) – and he was an only child, but that, he decided, proved nothing. He had never thought to ask her which was the more painful. Either way, it hurt like hell. He pulled up when the road was wide enough to park in a sliver of shade. He was in another village street, opposite another village store and a pub, this time separate buildings. He wound up the driver's side window and rested his right temple against its coldness.

Ritter knew, although a chain of neurologists his news editor had sent him to on the recommendation of the *Post*'s medical editor would not agree, that the attack had nothing to do with the excitement or frustration of the job, nor with the brilliant sunshine, nor with the double gin, nor even with last night's port and stilton. Something triggered a series of attacks; but nobody had been able to establish what, or why. The pain lasted exactly two hours each time, and it sometimes occurred as often as six times a day. The series could last six weeks or six months and the gaps in between could be three months or three years. He had suffered from it for twelve years now, since he was seventeen. When a cluster was in progress, Ritter had established that the pain was exacerbated by alcohol. Although a variety of foods – citrus fruit, milk products especially chocolate and cheese, beef extracts, red wine, and game – were all causes of classic migraines, between attacks nothing he ate or drank seemed to make the slightest difference.

But right now it hurt like hell. It hurt like a drill bit or a skewer being turned slowly through and behind the right eye. It hurt like a carpenter's vice being tightened slowly across half the head. Half the head – the name of the pain came from the Greek *hemicrania*: if the pain covered the whole head it was simply a headache.

There was nothing to do, now, until the pain stopped in two hours' time. Ritter checked his watch: it was twenty to two. In London the newsroom would be deserted, save for one man covering the news desk phones. The lads would be drinking cooking bitter in the 'downstairs office', also known as the Glue Pot. Nobody called it by its proper name, the Swan With Two Necks, the one chosen by the brewers rather than by the drinkers. More discerning palates would be down at the Ye Olde Cheshire Cheese drinking real ale and maybe planning to eat. It needed little planning: it was either Ye Famous Roast Beef or Ye Famous Steak And Kidney Pudding. Except in summer, defined in impeccably optimistic English logic as April to September, when ye steak and kidney pudding was replaced by Ye Famous Steak And Kidney Pie. He'd have to skip his visits until the migraine stopped. Even the braised onions and braised leeks that had first attracted him there were nothing without the Marston's bitter to wash them down.

This attack would stop at twenty to four, precisely, after which he would feel well enough to drive on. His head would still feel as though he'd gone five rounds with Henry Cooper, but a simple Anadin would help clear that. He always carried Anadin in the glove compartment, with his spare cigarettes and lighters.

He shifted his position to find a new cold spot on the window and eventually moved his temple to rest against the chrome brightwork of the quarter-light frame. His right eye was closed, and weeping, but he was aware, through his left, of a figure emerging from the village store on the opposite side of the road. It did not move down the street, as he might have expected. Instead it came up to his window, providing temporary respite from the light.

Through the open rear window a voice asked whether he was all right. Ritter wiped the tears from his eye and looked up.

'I'm OK, really, I'm afraid I'm suffering from migraine.'

It was a woman, perhaps in her late sixties or early seventies. In the heat of the day she was wearing a navy blue shawl over a bottle green twin set and maroon skirt.

'Would you like to come in for a cup of tea? Would that help? I live just here.' There was a hint of a long-forgotten accent, not Irish. She indicated the doorstep on the nearside of the Rapier. 'Or perhaps a cold drink?'

Ritter blew his nose, which always streamed when he had the pain, and again he wiped his weeping eye. He reached for the Rothmans on his front passenger seat; he never moved without them.

'A cold drink – just water, anything like that – would be fine, thank you.'

'Please leave the cigarettes. We don't smoke in our house.'

Compliantly, Ritter followed her into her home. After the piercing sunlight he found the house pleasantly gloomy. It was not heated by the sunshine, and a coal and peat fire burned in the grate.

In what appeared to be a two-up, two-down (kitchen and living room) terraced town house, there was one window looking out on to the street, and beneath it a table covered by a chenille, tasselled, cloth of old gold, at which sat a man of similar age to the woman who had brought Ritter indoors. Old pictures, photographs and watercolours of pre-war steamers and sailing ships, decorated the walls; Ritter noticed that, rather than hanging on picture hooks, they were attached to the wall by screws, as if the pictures themselves might once have been on board ships. Courteously, the man got slowly to his feet as the stranger entered.

'I thought I'd better bring this young man in.' She spoke slowly and deliberately, as if to intimate that she had not made the decision lightly. 'He's got migraine.'

'I can see that.' It was said matter-of-factly, not unkindly. The man who now invited him to sit down clearly was, or had been, a doctor. That much was immediately obvious by the way he gently took Ritter's wrist and measured his pulse. He lightly felt the arteries on each side of the neck, tested the forehead temperature with his fingertips, and peered into the right eye.

'What have you eaten today?' His voice was quiet, his speech clipped. His accent was much more pronounced than his wife's: *mittel-european*, Ritter decided, possibly Jewish. Yes; the man's shirt was buttoned to the neck, and he wore no tie. He was overweight and almost completely bald, with a round, full face, a brownish complexion with dark brown eyes behind thick glasses. His fingers were thick and his hands hairy. His fingernails, Ritter thought, looked in need of a good scrub.

'All I've had all day is a large G and T, no breakfast. But it's not that kind of migraine,' said Ritter. 'It's not an allergy. Not a reaction to food.'

'I know it's not. It's migrainous neuralgia. It comes in clusters, doesn't it?' Ritter nodded. Cluster headaches was the technical expression: the man knew what he was talking about.

'How long does each one last? About an hour?'

'Two. Exactly two.'

Ritter, his own eyes creased with the agony, noticed that there was something odd about the doctor's eyes. It was difficult for him to concentrate, but he eventually realised that when the doctor blinked, his eyes closed from the bottom upwards, something he was sure he had never seen before, although he had an idea that it was something that reptiles' eyes did. He tried to picture a lizard or tortoise: he was pretty sure that was how lizards' eyes closed. He also noticed that the doctor sweated profusely in the fireside heat, the wetness darkening his blue shirt beneath the armpits, across the upper chest, and down the middle of his back, and with each movement a fresh wave of body odour wafted towards Ritter. It was sharp, like ammonia. The doctor asked again what, if anything, he'd eaten, and nodded in response to the negative reply.

'And how many cigarettes do you think you've smoked today?'

'I don't know, maybe five.'

'And maybe ten,' said the doctor, turning over Ritter's palm and looking pointedly at the nicotine-stained fingertips. 'Maybe twenty. You should give it up.'

'I know. I've tried it. As Mark Twain said, "Any fool can give up smoking – I've done it a hundred times." But I sometimes feel that it helps the pain, because it keeps my breathing regular. At least, that's what I tell myself. That's my excuse.'

'Oh? Regular breathing helps? You think so? Or did your doctor tell you that?'

'I worked it out for myself. But... I don't know... maybe it's just an excuse for not giving up cigarettes.'

'No. It's very clever, very wise, very wise indeed. What helps, it helps only a little but it helps, are regular intakes of oxygen. The purer the better. Get fresh air inside you. It's excellent air here, for example. Anywhere in this village. But don't poison it with nicotine and tar. If you got your doctor to prescribe an oxygen cylinder, it might help. What has your doctor prescribed for this?'

'Only useless things, really, Valium, Librium, painkillers that don't work... they think that it's caused by stress or tension. Even the so-called specialists think it's depression or something. But they don't understand anything about it.'

'Oh? Why do you say that?'

'They can't understand the pain unless they suffer from it. If they suffer from it, they're no use because they can't cure themselves.'

The man sighed. 'Physician cure thyself, you mean? Or first remove the mote from thine own eye? It's a good argument, but a weak premise. If you think about it, not many gynaecologists have much personal experience of being women. Not many surgeons are amputees. Maybe helping you would help them cure their own ailments. Have you thought of that? – No... Let me take your blood pressure.'

Like the room in which he was sitting, the equipment looked oddly out of date. It was clean, the silver bits were even shiny, but the tin box produced by the doctor and the rubbery pieces he extracted from it looked, reasonably, to be of a similar vintage to that of the old man.

While the doctor pumped away at a rubber bulb, Ritter filled him in with more medical detail.

'The last specialist I went to was convinced I was suffering from depression. When I told him that I was well known among my colleagues for never being depressed about anything, he said that trying to live up to that image, of never being depressed, would have the same effect as being depressed in the first place. I told him that was just ball... balderdash. I couldn't get across to him that the only thing that was likely to depress me was the fact that doctors have no cure for this type of migraine. And if I dwelt on the matter, I guess that would depress the hell – the heck – out of me.'

'Did it have any effect, this anti-depressant course?'

'Not on the migraine...' Ritter refrained from mentioning that the one effect the drugs did have was to inhibit his sex life. Years earlier, as a bachelor with a flat overlooking the mouth of the Tyne, his flatmate had challenged girls they brought home: 'See what you can do for Ritter, will you? I'll bet that, whatever you do to him, he can't rise to the occasion.' Sadly for Ritter, the flatmate always won the bet.

Ritter had told his own GP about that. But here, after all, there was a lady present. And, in any case, the doctor nodded as if he understood the unmentioned problem. The lady in question had meanwhile brought a glass of iced water which, instead of drinking, Ritter pressed against his right temple. The ice cubes clinked against the glass. It brought a slight, but welcome, relief.

'I used to be a doctor, you know?' Ritter nodded and again brushed away the tears from his eye. 'But I'm retired now. I do have a preparation that I think can relieve your pain. Of course, I'm not legally permitted to prescribe it these days, but I have it here, and I believe it will work.' He looked questioningly at Ritter.

In days past, Ritter had seriously considered selling his soul to the devil in return for relief from the pain; certainly, he'd prayed and prayed with promises of renewed regular churchgoing if God – any god – could remove the agony.

'Please try it,' he said, 'if there's any chance at all that it will stop this pain.'

His wife – she carried herself like a former model or dancer, Ritter thought – brought a leather Gladstone bag to the table and the doctor easily found a hypodermic syringe and then rummaged about for a phial of the medicine, which he placed on the table's plush cover. He found a vein and pinched it, swabbed the area and inserted the needle. Ritter, who was used to pain but preferred not to watch, closed his eyes. They remained closed while he felt the pain ease away. Like a shovelful of snow held in front of a roaring fire, the pain quickly melted from the edges to the centre.

'Wow!' said Ritter, as he rolled down his shirtsleeve and refastened his cufflinks. 'Have you any more of that stuff?'

'I hope,' said the doctor, 'that you'll never need any again.'

*

Nature's single compensation for severe pain is that there is no complete memory of it. So Ritter drove on to Dublin with no recollection of the real torture he had experienced in the middle of the day. He knew, of course, that he'd had a migraine attack, and that it would have been one of a series and that it had been as severe as it ever was. But he was somehow already feeling adequately confident in the doctor to be sure that the migraine was, if anything, uniquely part of a cluster of only one. His head was now pain-free until the next spate of attacks. If there were any future attacks – the old doctor had said there might never be another, but that was too much to hope for. Anyway, Ritter was sufficiently assured and secure to order pints of Guinness when Kerrigan, one of the *Post*'s Dublin staff men, joined him at the bar of the Gresham in response to a request for some urgent local assistance and background.

'Sure, we'd like to help you on this,' said Kerrigan, his eyes blinking through the thick lenses of his heavy black-framed glasses. 'The trouble is knowing where to start. If we'd had any ideas on it at all, of course, we'd have tackled the job ourselves, you know, then there'd have been no need for London to send a BTO over on it.'

BTO meant Big-Time Operator. Kerrigan was feeling aggrieved, taking the piss a bit.

'All I want,' said Ritter, 'is a contact number for the IRA.'

Kerrigan looked astonished. He lowered his voice.

'A what! A contact number? For the IRA? The IRA doesn't exist, for Jesus' sake! You can't telephone it! It's an illegal organisation.'

'Great. It doesn't exist, but it's an illegal organisation. Is that what you're saying? Is that what you really mean?'

'I mean it isn't in the bloody phone book.'

'Well, what about Sinn Fein?'

'Sinn Fein? That's a proper political party, like your Labour Party. It's nothing to do with the IRA.'

'I thought it was the political front of the IRA. Bloody hell, they taught us that at school.'

'They don't teach it at schools here, matey. And don't you repeat it here or they'll... I don't know, they'll...'

'I know: Sinn Fein will get somebody to burn my bloody farm down. Look, you and Connolly are always writing stories about the IRA. What do you do for quotes when they' – Ritter racked his brains for recent IRA stories – 'when they blow up winning posts on race tracks, or pinch the rifle off some poor English squaddie? You must speak to somebody for them, unless you just make the quotes up.'

'God,' said Kerrigan, impervious to the professional insult. 'You English people... you never understand. The IRA contacts us. We don't ring them. There's never any contact from our direction, only from their side.'

'In that case,' said Ritter, 'ask them, next time they call, why they're blowing up foreign bloody farms. And tell them London wants the copy by lunch tomorrow.'

Ritter ate dinner alone in the ground floor dining room of the hotel founded a hundred and fifty years earlier by a Londoner, Thomas Gresham, simply because he had been unable to find anywhere decent to stay and to eat in the Irish capital. Also eating alone in the dining room was a dark stocky man whose cheerful Irish potato face looked faintly familiar. After racking his brain Ritter realised that the man opposite ordering hors d'oeuvre of cucumber with black pepper – 'it's amazing what you can get yourself used to,' he'd told the waiter with a smirk – was Sean Bourke. The man had claimed responsibility for freeing traitor George Blake from Wormwood Scrubs prison. At the end of the meal

Ritter crossed the floor to where Bourke was sitting. He stretched out his hand.

'Hello, my name's Ritter. I recognised you from over there. I wonder, can I buy you a drink, Mr Blake?'

'Mister... WHO?'

'Oh God, sorry.' Ritter laughed nervously. 'Sorry. I suppose that's what they call a Freudian slip. I meant Bourke, of course. An easy mistake, I suppose. My name's Ritter, from the *Post*.'

'Bloody awful paper that is. Never get their facts right. Most of the stuff they did on the Blake escape they got wrong. Bloody rubbish reporters, your lot.' He eyed Ritter mischievously. 'You are a reporter, are you?'

'Wrong?' said Ritter. 'You think we got things wrong? It wasn't half as wrong as the book you wrote with your supposed account of the actual escape. What a load of bollocks that was. I could have written it better myself. As a matter of fact, I was on that job and I did write it better myself!'

Bourke grinned. 'You're right. Sit down,' he said. 'The *Post*'s was the best coverage, I'd say. Let's have a drink.' He raised his hand to summon a waiter.

*

Ritter woke, fully clothed, on the quilt of his double bed in the Gresham. He never suffered from hangovers (in fact one theory he'd concocted was that his occasional bouts of migraine were actually all his accumulated hangovers, saved up for months) but he knew he'd had a drink. Some red wine, or port, or both − but there'd been at least a bottle of it − had been involved. And some brandy, or maybe Irish whiskey. Or both. Something he'd never have done during a migraine cluster. He had a vague recollection of walking up O'Connell Street with his arm round the shoulder of someone much shorter than himself. Bourke's shoulder? Possibly. Of going into a block of flats, riding in a lift, and Bourke, or whoever his companion was, ringing the bell. He remembered waiting for the bell to be answered, but didn't remember the door's opening. He seemed to think that this had all happened about four in the morning.

He checked his watch. It was ten o'clock. Not much time to sort out the IRA farm bombs story. As well as his watch he saw a piece of paper, lined, but not torn from his notebook. He quickly checked: his notebook was in his jacket pocket. That was reassuring; a reporter would rather lose his wallet than his notebook: the wallet usually had less in it. Scribbled on the paper, but not in his own handwriting, was a six-figure number, the ballpoint ink slightly blurred by sweat from his palm. It looked like a phone number, so he picked up the phone, asked reception for a line, and dialled it.

'Hello...'

'Er, is that Mr Bourke?'

'Sorry, wrong number.'

A flash of inspiration: 'No – sorry,' he said quickly, before the person attached to the voice could hang up. 'Just a moment, er, it was Mr Bourke gave me the number, and... is that, er, is that the IRA?' God, he felt amateurish!

'Who's calling?'

'My name's Ritter, from the *Post*, the newspaper, in London. A friend of Sean Bourke.'

The man stayed on the line. Ritter told him what he wanted – needed – to know, and the strange voice explained, in considerable detail, that the Irish were opposed to foreigners buying up their best agricultural land and pushing the prices beyond the pockets of native Irishmen. They were content for foreign investors to bring industry in to areas of unemployment but opposed to any outsiders actually owning good Irish soil. It was sometimes necessary, he said, to take some unpleasant action to make this point, and to deter new buyers.

At the end of the interview Ritter asked the speaker's name and was told that while he could quote the man, he couldn't name him. When Ritter promised that he wanted the name only for his own assurance, not for publication, he was given the name. He asked for the man's connection with the IRA.

'So long as you don't put it in the paper.'

'Of course.' Ritter was scrupulous about such arrangements with his informants and contacts, even with those he hadn't actually met.

'I'm the Chief of Staff...'

Ritter rang his office.

'I've got the story − straight from the horse's mouth − from the IRA... from the Chief of Staff,' he told the news editor.

'Did you have to get Kerrigan to help you?'

'He says he doesn't know anybody in the IRA.'

'Who did you speak to, then?'

'I told you. I've just spoken to the top man in the IRA, at his home.'

'Kinnell!' It was a favourite curse. 'How did you find him?'

'Sort of friend of a friend, I suppose. As a matter of fact, I went round to his place, the top feller's, the number one, last night with Sean Bourke − you know, the guy who got Blake out.' No need to say there'd been nobody in.

'Kinnell! Nice one. File it, and come home.'

Ritter was transferred to a copytaker to whom he dictated his story. He waited an hour and then checked with the news desk that they had got it and had no queries for him. Then he rang and asked reception to prepare his bill.

All without getting out of − or at least without getting off − the bed.

*

All newspapers have libraries and some, obviously, are better than others; the *Post*'s was reputed to be one of the best in the Street. They are the places where newspapers are cut and stories filed under subject and personality headings, so that a story like Ritter's would be filed under *IRA* and *Ireland – Republic – Agriculture*, as well as *Ireland-German relations* and also under *Terrorism*, and *Ireland – law and order*, and then also under *Ritter-copy*.

Newspaper libraries bear no resemblance to public reading rooms; there are no places to sit and browse, no access to desks or tables, merely a counter with trays for the collection and return of manila envelopes and buff-coloured folders full of cuttings; and, beyond the counter, row after row of filing cabinets and shelves. But there is available virtually every known reference book, and it was to the *Post*'s library that Ritter sent an editorial assistant (a modern name for a copyboy) to fetch him the medical directories for the United Kingdom and Ireland.

It had occurred to him, recounting his experience in the Glue Pot, that he did not know the name of the kindly doctor who had relieved – possibly cured – his migraines. So he found a number for the nearest *Gardai* station, rang it, and described the house opposite the village grocer's shop.

'That would be Mr and Mrs Morell,' said the policeman.

'Doctor and Mrs,' Ritter corrected, automatically.

'No, I don't think he's a doctor at all.'

'He used to be.'

'I wouldn't think so.'

Ritter described the doctor and his wife; there was no doubt that they were talking about the same people. Yet the local policeman did not know he had a doctor, even a retired doctor, in the next village.

Stranger was the discovery that the Morells were not on the telephone: doctors, even retired doctors, were always on the telephone. Ritter wanted to write, although he would have preferred to phone, and thank the doctor, but he decided first to check the full name and address. Again, he drew blanks. And this, because of his reporter's training, irritated him. There was no real need to check the name and address: he had them from the *Gardai*, but not being able to find a doctor in a reference book was an annoyance.

He remembered that Mrs Morell had called her husband 'Teddy', so he was looking for Doctor Edward Morell, now aged, Ritter guessed, between 70 and 80. It was impossible for a doctor to be unfindable through reference books.

Another clue occurred to him as he drove to work one morning: the bottle from which Doctor Morell had drawn the injection had been labelled Merck. The paper's medical editor was starting his daily chore of opening and reading a few dozen press releases when Ritter's lanky frame loomed over his desk and he explained his quest.

'That's interesting, Merck,' said Alan McDairmid. 'Merck is probably the oldest pharmaceutical company in the world. Dates back to something like the 1660s, when the original Merck took over the slightly older Engel Pharmacy in Darmstadt. After the First World War they split, and half the company became Merck Sharp and Dohme, whose parent company is American, the other half is Merck, Darmstadt, which is of course German. But they're not in England, the ones just called Merck, so the chance is that the bottle you saw was Merck Sharp and Dohme.'

'Nope. It just said Merck. And I think it might even have said Engel, too.'

'I think that's unlikely, but if you're sure about that, you're talking about German medicine, not British. It often happens with European medicines that you can buy them over the counter there, but they're available only on prescription here. On the other hand, there are medicines there that aren't available at all here, and some that have a similar counterpart in the UK but that are not quite the same combination of contents. Not the same formula. So what you're looking for is a doctor who buys his medicine on the

Continent because he's struck off, or maybe because he can't prescribe for some other reason.'

'Or because he's a retired German doctor,' said Ritter, remembering the accent. 'He's not struck off, I've checked back in British medical directories from before the war, a time when he'd certainly be practising: there's nobody in *Black's* between Moreland and Moreton. He isn't in any of them.'

'A German doctor?' said McDairmid. 'Maybe the embassy can help.'

But the West German embassy was also unable to trace a Doctor Edward Morell, so Ritter rang the headquarters of the Axel Springer group in Hamburg and spoke to Hermann Bayer, a German reporter he had met who had been covering the Aberfan tip disaster for *Die Welt*.

When Bayer called back it was to say that there was no Edward Morell qualifying in Germany, either.

'But we have a T.G. Morell, Theodor Gilbert. Could it be that your Eddy is a Teddy, you know, like Roosevelt? This guy was born in July '86, matriculated at Giessen, read medicine at Heidelberg, studied in Paris and Grenoble, licensed as a medical practitioner by the Royal Bavarian State Ministry – that is of course in Munich – under section 29 of the Reich Professional Code, in May 1913. I am reading from my notes, in case you haven't realised. He was an assistant doctor first at Bad Kreuznach, then a ship's doctor with various shipping lines including the North German Lloyd lines—'

'A ship's doctor?' Ritter suddenly remembered the pictures on the wall.

'That's right... then he had a practice in Dietzenbach – that's near Offenbach – until the First World war, then he bought a practice in Bayreutherstrasse, in Berlin. In 1935 he bought a posh surgery in the Kurfurstendamm where, basically, he was a pox doctor for the arty set. He married an actress, in fact. A good looker, considering he was an ugly fat bugger himself.'

Got 'em! thought Ritter. 'You know a lot about him.'

'There's a lot to know. In his days on the Ku-damm he was as well-known as a coloured dog.' Bayer paused, and Ritter took the opportunity to translate the simile into German – *bekannt wie ein bunter hund* – and back out again, in a vain effort to make sense of it.

'Coloured dog? What are you talking about?'

'OK: perhaps spotted dog, like a Dalmatian... it means prominent in the area... Er, I say, Ritter, how much of this stuff do you want?'

'Where is he supposed to be now?'

The young German laughed. 'You serious? Your guess is as good as mine. Hell, probably.'

'Where do you mean? Hell in Norway?'

'Norway no way! Hell as in Hades. It's more likely than Heaven, I'd say. You know of course that he died.'

'He died?'

'In April 1945. When Hitler told him to get out of the bunker.'

'Hitler?' said Ritter, incredulously. 'You mean he was in the bunker with Hitler?'

'Seriously, Ritter,' said Bayer, 'I'd assumed you knew that, and you were just playing silly buggers, English-style, and going a roundabout way of asking about him, and eventually getting to the point. Are you taking the piss? He was in the underground shelter beneath the Reich Chancellery at the end. I mean the very end. He was there, either there or in Berchtesgaden or Rastenberg, in fact wherever Hitler was, from about 1937 to the end.'

'What was he doing, exactly?'

'Exactly? He was the Führer's *Leibarzt* – his personal physician – of course!'

'Oh shi-i-i-it,' shouted Ritter. 'Save everything you've got on him. I'll be over there tonight, if there's a plane.'

*

Ritter, who had left a warm late spring day in London, flew into a winter's night in Hamburg with icy wind whipping around the aircraft steps. Hermann Bayer, a dapper little man, slight as a jockey, who bought his trendy suits whenever a foreign job took him within reach of London's Carnaby Street, had ventured into Jermyn Street on his most recent shopping spree and now his Beatle-mopped head appeared to be mounted on the matching fur collar of a Burberry-style trench coat. He greeted Ritter at the airport and pointedly showed him how to adjust the legroom to get more space in the front passenger seat of his red Audi coupe, then they drove to the Springer building in Kaiser Wilhelm Strasse with *Eleanor Rigby* booming on the in-car stereo.

'Why can't you krauts try something moderate for a change, like a moderate temperature?' Ritter asked, while adjusting the Audi's heating controls. 'Why do you do everything in extremes, whether it's the politics or the climate? It's bloody freezing!'

'You know that we have a full range of everything in our country. We have all European geography, and so we have all the European weather to go with it. That is why our country is so beautiful, and our climate so varied. Instead of hating it and its people, as you do, you should grow to love it; it encompasses everything European.'

'You know,' said Ritter, 'when God was creating Europe, he got all the different geographical bits in a pile. He said, "Here's some mountains and fjords; I'll put these at the top and call it Scandinavia. Here's a flat bit, I'll put this over here and call it Netherlands." He had some rolling moors, that he called Britain and Ireland, some alps, that he called Switzerland, a long string of hills and coastline, that he made Italy, and so on. When he'd finished he found he had bits of everything left over – hills and dales, moors and mountains and alps, pretty coastlines, plains and forests and rivers. He didn't know what to do with it, so he dumped it smack in the centre and called it Germany. Well, all the other countries protested that while they had only one or two features each, Germany had everything. God saw it wasn't fair and said he would think of a way to equalise it. "I know," he said eventually. "I'll make the bloody Germans live there! That'll make it right."

'God knows,' said Ritter, in case Bayer had missed the point, 'You're a miserable bunch of bastards.'

Together they jumped on to a paternoster lift and rode up to the editorial floor. Bayer had recently been appointed an assistant editor, and had his own comfortably furnished office. There were stacks of documents spread across his desk and along the office sofa, all waiting for Ritter's attention, many of them already photocopied so that he could take them away.

'What's all this interest in a dead man?' It was a reasonable question, especially in view of the amount of work Bayer had clearly put in to the exercise. That, plus the fact that Ritter had seen fit to jump on a plane to Hamburg at a moment's notice.

Ritter was only slightly embarrassed. 'Look, Hermann, I can't tell you yet. But if it works out, I promise you'll be the first to know.'

'Tell me now, Ritter, and I'll help you dig it up. Morell was a German and in the Hitler bunker, and there's a lot of interest here for Hitler stories – more, probably, even than in England.'

'There isn't a story yet, Hermann. Just leave me with it. I'll let you know.'

'If you can come shooting across from England at the drop of a hat, there must already be something.'

'Yes, but it's something and nothing at the moment. Look, I'll see you get some money for this, for the work you've done. But, at the moment, I don't know what there is to it, or even if it's the man I'm looking for.'

*

In his bedroom at the Atlantic hotel, with an ice-cold Alster lake beneath his double-glazed windows, Ritter pieced together the story of Morell's life. The picture that emerged was of a conceited, cunning, avaricious man, dirty in his habits, and despised by all around him. By all, that is, except the Führer.

The two men had been introduced by Heinrich Hoffmann, Hitler's personal photographer, who Morell had apparently been treating for gonorrhoea. Hoffmann asked the doctor to join him in Munich and Morell agreed, possibly because the Reich Chancellor sent his personal plane to collect him. Another member of the party had been a girl he knew only as Hoffmann's laboratory assistant, called Eva Braun.

While Morell treated the photographer, Hitler had asked him to look at the eczema in his legs. The doctor examined him and said he could, and would, cure him. From there it was a short step to becoming personal physician.

There was no doubt that, among other things, he produced seemingly miracle cures for the Führer's severe head pains, and no doubt in Ritter's mind that the doctor in the tiny run-down house in Ireland was the man who'd personally served Hitler in the bunker.

At the same time, there was no doubt in the sheaves of German archive material that Herr Professor Doctor Theodor Gilbert Morell was dead.

*

Ritter and Bill McKeown, his news editor, were almost unique in the *Post* office in that they were not Scottish. Ritter had been brought up on Tyneside and McKeown, although acknowledging Scots ancestry, was from Northern Ireland.

One common bond was their frequent repetition of a story told by Hannen Swaffer, the legendary reporter and editor,

who'd said there were too many Scotsmen in Fleet Street...
'So I put down bowls of poisoned porridge at Kings Cross
station – only the buggers defeated me by coming in to St
Pancras because the fare was a halfpenny cheaper!' The
Scots retaliated by describing both Geordies and Ulstermen
as 'Scotsmen with their brains kicked out'. It was what
passed as humour, north of the border.

McKeown had been in Berlin as a war correspondent in
1945 and consequently had an above-average interest in the
city and the period. He had been sceptical about sending his
reporter to Hamburg and now wanted a full report to justify
the expenditure, in readiness for an inquiry from the bean-
counters in editorial management.

'What's the proof that the doctor, Hitler's doctor, is
dead?'

'He came out of the bunker with Bormann and another
guy and they must have been hit by shrapnel from a Russian
shell. In any case, he was seen dead by Artur Axmann, the
Hitler Youth boss...'

'Reichsjugendführer.'

Ritter laughed: 'That's the word I was groping for. He
was found near the bridge where Invalidenstrasse crosses the
railway line not far from Friedrichstrasse station, lying on his
back.'

'There's no death certificate, though?'

'I don't think so. There was no inquest, either. Don't
forget, at the end of April, beginning of May '45, the
Russians were in Berlin pounding shit out of everything; they
certainly weren't picking up bodies and checking their IDs
against a missing persons list. They might have been picking
up bodies and shafting them, or nicking their watches and
wallets, but not much else.'

'You're telling me? I was there in Berlin at the end, you
know.'

So was I, Ritter thought to himself. But to McKeown he
said: 'Then I don't have to tell you, do I? Anyway, you war

correspondents obviously arrived well after the Russians, and the whole point is that he didn't die; he's in Ireland. So the first question is how did he get there?'

'That's not the first question. The first question is what's the proof that Hitler's doctor is your doctor?'

'There's his name, for a start. Pretty conclusive, wouldn't you say? Hitler's quack is Theodor Morell, mine is Teddy Morell. Teddy is Theodore, as in Theodore Roosevelt equals Teddy Roosevelt. There's no doctor called Edward or Teddy Morell in the UK or Ireland, or, come to that, anywhere else but Germany. And even in Germany there's no Morell after 1945.'

'But you've got only an Irish copper's word for it that he's called Morell.'

'He got it from the electoral roll, the voters' list, but he knew them anyway by my description.'

'What if he's a different kind of doctor? For all you know he might be a doctor of music, or divinity, or philosophy. Three of those kraut farmers you went looking for called themselves doctor. Two degrees and they call themselves *Herr doktor-doktor.*'

'Oh. Come on, Bill! You can tell a doctor's way of taking your pulse, and giving injections, and all that. In any case, he said he was, or had been, a doctor. And he had all the kit; I don't think it's for playing doctors and nurses with his missus. And besides, he knew so much. He is a doctor, medical type, right enough.'

'OK. Let's chance it so far. Get back to see him, and if it stands up get him to talk. Kinnell! It'll run and run, this one... We'll do the mystery, the escape, how you found him, life in the bunker, and life with his pal Adolf, and what, medically, made the Führer the way he was, and then life in hiding for twenty years. The TV will love it, too, give us maximum exposure. It won't do the Irish drive any harm, either.'

McKeown was silent for a moment, a professional, already picturing the words and pictures on the page. 'I tell you; this'll run for weeks. You can retire on it. Get on to pictures; tell them you want to take an artist in light and shade with you. It could cover its own costs in syndication alone: this story'll sell round the world if it stands up.'

He paused again, frowning. He had pulled off his glasses and was chewing on the frame, a recognisable sign to his reporters that he was excited. 'No, look: on second thoughts, it is big. I don't want you to talk to anybody else about this. Ring me every day at, say, four o'clock. Let me know how it's going. If I'm not on the desk, leave a message asking me to ring you back. Don't tell anybody else where you are or what you're up to. This building leaks like a fucking sieve. Don't even tell the boss.'

'Hey, come off it, Bill! If the editor asks what I'm up to, I've got to tell him.'

'No you haven't. Just say you're doing a special for me. And if he wants to know the details, to ask me. I've got a feeling in my bones about this one. If anybody asks, anybody at all, I'll say you're on a job in... where?'

Ritter thought for a moment. 'Dunkirk.' He seemed to have plucked the place out of the air. 'But why don't I see if Doctor Morell will talk, first?'

*

'I think Tex is on to a stormer.' It was eight o'clock and the *Post*'s first edition was being made up in the second floor composing room. As was his habit, Bill McKeown had gone into the office of managing editor Jake Morris to discuss the day and generally 'unwind' over a few glasses of Scotch. Ritter was known to a few intimates as 'Tex' Ritter, in honour of the singing cowboy of early talkies, who had also recorded the title song of *High Noon*.

'We think he's found Hitler's doctor, a chap called Morell, who's supposed to be dead, only he's alive and well and living in hiding in Ireland.'

'Bugger me, cock! Are we staking the place out?'

'Not yet. Tex found him by accident and the old quack seems to have cured his headaches. He didn't know who he was then, but it's checked out and it looks like it's standing up. There's bill for a return ticket to Hamburg in the system. I don't want any questions asked about it, when it surfaces.'

'Does the law know?'

'Nobody knows, yet. He's got to see how it pans out. As far as we know, the law isn't looking for him. We haven't even told pictures.'

'Who has been told?'

'Nobody.'

'Perfect. Let's try and keep this one under wraps.'

*

'One of my boys is working on a good 'n', Morris confided as he cut in to a lamb chop in the dining room of the Reform Club. 'We think he's found Hitler's personal doctor.'

'Not Morell.'

'That's him.'

'No. Not Morell: Morell's dead.'

'That's the point! He was supposed to be dead in 1945. But we've found him alive.'

'Morell wasn't a war criminal, you know.'

'Wasn't he?'

'Not at all. He was cleared, posthumously.'

'Cleared posthumously? Why would anybody want to do a thing like that?'

'Now you mention it, I can't think why anybody would want to bother to clear a dead man. But I suppose it helps the family, they may have asked for it. Most of the others in the bunker were topped at the end of the war. There were so many German doctors in the late 1940s who were war criminals it might have been fairly reasonable to announce that one dead man wasn't involved in the so-called experiments. Morell wasn't involved at all.'

'Every bastard in the SS was a war criminal, by definition,' said Morris.

'In theory, yes. In law, yes. But then Morell wasn't in the SS.'

*

At the annual general meeting of the OK Korrall Klub of Hamburg, Otto 'Wyatt' Mucher was elected marshall and Heinz 'Doc' Flemm elected as his deputy. As the two celebrated their appointments at a woodlands bar, Flemm, an assistant librarian in the Springer organisation, bemoaned the fact that, more than twenty years after the war, people were still interested in old comrades with remote connections with the Berlin bunker such as Doctor Morell. When he had finished his drink, Mucher wished his new deputy a good night and stopped off on the way home to call on an old army friend.

TWO

Doctor Morell's face was ivory white. His green shirt darkened with sweat across his upper chest as his anger rose.

'We did not need to invite you in to our home. My wife invited you in as a stranger and we tried to help you!' He was shouting. 'We tried to relieve your pain! We behaved towards you as a friend! And how do you repay this? You return to our home as a viper! With vile assertations! With scandalous slanders!'

Ritter was slightly embarrassed by the doctor's outburst, but only slightly. He was ready to make a grovelling apology to the couple if he was wrong. But he felt sure he was right, and the more the doctor ranted, the surer was Ritter that Hitler's doctor was only posturing over him in the snug sitting room of the tiny Irish house. The gut feeling was aided by the fact that Doctor Morell protested about the accusation, not against it. What Morell was complaining about was that Ritter was accusing him – but not that the accusation was wrong.

Mrs Morell had, in fact, greeted him at the door as an old friend. She had taken his hand and invited him in.

'Look who's here, Teddy,' she called to her husband. 'I'll just put the kettle on.'

Doctor Morell's face at first clouded in doubt. 'Your migraine – it hasn't come back?'

'Not at all. I wanted to thank you. In a funny sort of way that's why I'm here.'

And as the doctor cheered up Ritter deflated him by explaining that his attempt to telephone and thank him for his seemingly miraculous cure had led to deep research into the last days of the War. At the first mention of his name, when Ritter had addressed him as Dr Morell – as if the mention of it brought back lost memories – he had begun to pale. By the time Ritter mentioned the surgery on the Kurfurstendamm, Morell was silently shaking. At the mention of the bunker, he was shouting. And his wife, teapot in hand, started sobbing.

'I'm sorry', said Ritter, sincerely. 'I'm sorry that what started as your kindness has led me back here. Of course, you couldn't have known I was a reporter, but at the time that had nothing to do with anything. You can deny it, if you like. If you tell me that you did something else during the war, that you were somewhere else... that you were some*one* else, then I'll happily check it out. Honestly. And see where we go from there.'

The couple paused while the possible implications of that suggestion sank in. 'We don't have to say anything,' ventured Mrs Morell. 'And if we don't, you can't write anything. You can't prove anything. Can he, Teddy?'

'Well it's true that I can't prove anything beyond doubt. I've no idea whether there are any fingerprints or that sort of thing still existing from twenty-odd years ago. But we can get a photograph of you somehow, then and now. You can't stay indoors for the rest of your lives, and it will look worse if you try to avoid having a photograph taken... If I can't prove anything, I can at least print what I know. I mean, I'd hate to resort to that sort of thing, but, if you drove me to it... The effect of that – right or wrong – will be to bring reporters and photographers and TV cameramen in to surround this place and stake it out, as we call it, until you do talk. And probably not to leave, even then. Your lives, for the rest of your lives, will be a misery. And it will be your fault for not talking to me now. Even if I'm wrong... which I know I'm not. I'm sorry.'

'How do you know you're not wrong? Why are you so sure?'

'Because you could have said "Hitler? Bunker? Don't be bloody ridiculous!" And instead you asked how I dared talk about it.'

Morell took his wife's small bony hands in his flabby palms and said he was taking her upstairs to talk in private. As the couple walked towards the staircase he glared at Ritter with hatred in his eyes and, almost under his breath, mouthed the word 'bastard!' Ritter realised that the doctor's eyes, and his wife's, were full of tears. Bayer's description had been right enough. Morell was an ugly fat bastard, and his wife was an ex-actress, if ever he'd seen one.

It was quiet in the room where the reporter sat alone, not disturbed even by the ticking of a clock. Nor was there any sound from upstairs.

Oh God! thought Ritter, sitting at the table under the window; I hope they haven't gone to get the cyanide tablets.

He poured himself a cup of lukewarm tea, and waited.

The creak of a stair tread roused Ritter from his thoughts. He looked up and found Morell once more standing over him.

'All these people you said would come, to besiege the house. It would kill my wife, you know. We are no longer young. What I want to say is, if we tell you what you want to know, we will have to make conditions, and you will have to agree and perhaps sign a paper before we talk.'

'You mean if you talk about your life in the bunker with Hitler, you want conditions?'

'Precisely.'

Ritter smiled. 'Tell me your conditions. If they're reasonable I'll agree. But you must realise that what you've just said amounts, in effect, to an admission in any case. Trust me though; I'll do what I can to help. We're all on the same side here.'

There was only one condition the Morells sought: that Ritter did not give any clue to their whereabouts. This suited the reporter perfectly – he didn't want any other newspaper to trace the couple. The idea of the little house being under siege by Fleet Street horrified him almost as much as it did the Morells, but for different reasons. But that was not a confidence he wanted to share with the German couple.

'It's the Israelis,' explained Doctor Morell. 'They mustn't be allowed to find us. We might not live much longer, but we want to live in peace, if we can.'

Heini Hoffmann, began Morell, *was a widower, and after the death of his wife he became a little, well, promiscuous. I did not specialise at my surgery in the Ku-damm, but quite a lot of my patients, though rich, were... Bohemian, they were loose-livers, and it became known that I would treat certain... diseases with discretion, and without pain. So he came to me for treatment. Heini was the Führer's – the Reich Chancellor's – personal photographer. He went everywhere with him, even on holiday.*

When we first met, the Führer already had a doctor, Brandt, who was a young surgeon and a Nazi. He treated Hitler's niece after a car accident in 1933, and the Führer was satisfied with him and made him his 'personal surgeon'. But this was a waste of time because the Führer never needed surgery, and when he was ill Brandt didn't know how to begin treating anything. And he worried about leaving all his rich patients and the clinic on Ziegelstrasse, so he brought in Professor von Hasselbach, another surgeon, as his deputy. That was ridiculous: two surgeons for a man who was hardly ever ill. And Brandt wasn't too busy to leave his practice when he was offered the Reich Commission for Health and Sanitation. He was dismissed from all offices, later, when the Führer learned that Brandt had sent his wife away from Berlin to a place where he knew she would be captured by the American army. As the Führer said, Brandt had lost all faith in victory. He was tried by a court and condemned to death. Bormann – who hated Brandt, we all hated Brandt, because he was no good as a doctor and he criticised my prescriptions – had him removed to a condemned cell in Kiel. He wasn't executed then, but he was tried by the Allies and executed for war crimes. I never heard what happened to Hasselbach.

So, I was treating Hoffmann for... er... pyelitis – I cured him; there were no complications – and once he needed me when he was at his villa in Bogenhausen, in the very elegant part of Munich. I didn't want to go, God knows, I had sufficient patients in Berlin. But the Führer – the Chancellor – felt it important enough to send his personal aircraft for me, so I went. In the event, I stayed there a month, including a trip to Venice where he went to convalesce.

Morell paused to ensure that Ritter was finding his story sufficiently interesting to be keeping pace with his shorthand note. Apparently satisfied, he continued:

That Christmas we were invited to spend the holiday with Heini Hoffmann and his new wife. On Christmas Day we drove up to the Obersalzburg mountains where Hitler lived in the Berghof and we were invited back every day.

One day we were sitting in the bowling alley on the seat around the fireplace when the Führer suddenly came in and asked whether I could spare a minute. We went in to the conservatory and he showed me the eczema on his legs. They were bandaged so much that he couldn't get his boots on. He also had stomach cramps. And Brandt hadn't been able to do a thing about either. I knew I could cure him, and the Führer even said he'd give us a new house if it worked!

It was the worst day of my life, as it turned out. I had a successful practice in Berlin, and we always had beautiful homes. I wanted for nothing. But that day changed everything. I wish it had never happened. I wish I'd never met him! We both wish I'd never met him! But I decided to take him on. I promised I'd have him healthy again in less than a year, and I knew I could do it.

'It wasn't the money or anything like that,' Mrs Morell interrupted, proudly. 'Teddy had already turned down offers as personal doctor to the Shah of Persia and the King of Romania. He treated the Crown Prince – he gave him a signed photo. His patients included Richard Tauber, the boxer Max Schmeling... He treated opera singers and ballet dancers and famous film actors and actresses, and of course politicians. And when he started looking after Hitler, even greater people came. And he treated Krupp and Thyssen, Goering, Goebbels, Albert Speer. He treated Hess...'

She looked at her husband as though for permission to continue, to break a confidence. Morell nodded.

'You know, when Hess flew to Scotland to talk to the English government, Teddy gave him some multi-vitamins to strengthen him on the journey. We never said anything about it, until now.'

I bet you didn't, thought Ritter, who was scribbling furiously.

'There was the Czech President, Hacha, who had a heart attack. And Mussolini. Even Neville Chamberlain, who had flu when he came to see Hitler in September 1938. Teddy treated him, too.'

'I remember him waving the prescription when he came back,' said Ritter, flippantly. He immediately wished he hadn't, because the Morells looked at him without comprehension, but Frau Morell continued unperturbed.

'And Jews. You treated a lot of Jews, didn't you, Teddy?'

I treated so many, the Nazis daubed the word Jude *across the nameplate outside my surgery. But I continued to treat my Jewish patients, even after that. Even after I joined the Party in – I don't know – in something like 1933. Anyway, I was one of the first. I only stopped when I became the Führer's Leibarzt, full time, and I had to drop all my private patients and appoint a deputy to run the surgery. I started my treatment and after six months the cramps had gone and he could eat normally again. Then after nine months the eczema had gone. The Führer said to me that I had promised to do it in a year, and I had done it even sooner. He said I was a miracle worker. Until he came to me, he was starving on only tea and biscuits. The other doctors didn't have a clue. The Führer just got thinner and thinner. He could hardly walk. They all gave him the wrong treatment. But I cured him!*

'What was he like?'

As a patient? He was very difficult. He seemed to suffer from a lot of ailments, while claiming that he had never been ill in his life. He'd had a polyp removed from his vocal chords, which sometimes gave him a sore throat.

Apart from that most of his problems were hysterical − especially the stomach cramps, which he'd had almost all his life. He suffered a lot from flatulence, but that was mainly because he was a vegetarian. He ate only vegetables and fruit, no meat, and for a time not even eggs. Sometimes his stomach was so tight and full of air that when I tapped it, it sounded like a drum. I had to give him things to remove the excess wind. He also suffered from frequent colds. So when he felt one coming on, I would give him a prophylactic, something which lifted his spirits, but more often than not it was a placebo: the Führer felt better after taking even an insignificant dose.

He sweated a lot, more than most people, but he wore moisture-absorbing pads in his armpits and beneath his collar so that the perspiration didn't show and so his shirt didn't stain and spoil his uniforms. And also from headaches. He suffered from the most blinding headaches...

Morell looked pointedly at Ritter, meaning to draw his attention to his reference to headaches; Ritter had noted it but was busily contemplating Hitler and Morell sweating in each other's company. It was a pity, Ritter thought, that Morell's boss had not shared his sweat-absorbing pads with his physician.

...But I was of course able to do something about that.

'Morphine?' The only drug Ritter knew that could relieve pain as quickly as Morell had relieved his own was morphine.

'Not morphine, exactly: morphine relieves, but it doesn't cure. And of course morphine introduces its own problems...'

Morell was starting on a new tack: 'When I first met him, he was like an old man. But by 1939 he was looking younger and fitter than his years.'

But Ritter wasn't finished: 'What drugs did you give him?'

'The names don't matter. But it probably averaged one injection a day over the nine or so years I was with him.'

'He must have been like a pin cushion,' Ritter suggested, recalling Bayer's note about Goering's calling Morell the 'master of the imperial needle'.

Morell merely shrugged. 'Injection is frequently the best way of administering drugs.'

'Why don't you give me a list of the medicines? Our readers are very interested in health, these days.'

'People want only to criticise. I got this from Brandt, and Hasselbach, and from Haase who came in between, and even from Giesling who was an ear specialist who came after the July bomb. They went to the Führer and said I was poisoning him with strychnine and belladonna. But when I showed that it was a proprietary drug called Dr Koester's Anti-Gas Pills, those who had been criticising me were all thrown out. The Führer recognised their jealousy for what it was. That was about the last time we saw Brandt and Hasselbach, and the Führer stopped calling Giesling in.'

'Not morphine, then? You weren't prescribing morphine?'

'Not so much morphine. That's addictive, as you know. But morphine substitutes.'

Ritter asked: 'Is that what you gave me? Whatever it was, it certainly seems to have worked.'

I told you: the names don't matter. All that counts is whether they work. People complain about the names, as though it's more important than the treatment. But when Himmler lent his doctor, Professor Gebhardt, an SS Obergruppenführer, to treat Speer, Speer only got worse: the treatment aggravated the condition. It was designed to. I knew that. Himmler wanted him dead. But Gebhardt became President of the German Red Cross after that. He was arrested for war crimes for carrying out experiments on girls in Auschwitz, and finally executed after confessing to the mass murder of ninety thousand Jews. Ninety thousand! So much for medicine. So much for treatment. So much for the Red Cross!

But when I said I would talk to you, that's not the same as giving you the prescriptions. All doctors disagree. I don't want them to conclude that after everything else, including saving the life of the Führer, I was an incompetent practitioner...

The doctor, interrupted only occasionally by his wife, talked on through the night. Ritter realised that he had burst a dam of consciousness that the couple had held back for two decades. He had filled half a dozen notebooks with recollections in Pitman's shorthand. And as the daylight came in through the sash window and fell across the gold plush tablecloth, he rubbed his eyes and decided to take a break.

Ritter now felt sufficiently confident in the belief that, if he left the house, the couple would wait for his return. Twelve hours earlier he would have been unsure: but by morning he knew that he was now an extension of their life;

they needed to tell their story, and now that they had started they had to tell it to him.

He crossed the road and sat in the car and went straight to sleep. The morning's traffic – a solitary farm tractor – woke him about six o'clock and he went for a walk to relieve his aching muscles. As soon as he noticed signs of life he booked in to the only guest room at the pub beside the village store. He asked for a call at nine o'clock, the time McKeown normally came into the office.

He felt awful. He couldn't remember the last time he'd had a cigarette. He had forgotten to tell Morell that he'd stopped smoking, purely as a consequence of his first visit. The old quack had probably noticed, but he would be proud to be told that. He asked for a glass of iced water, and drank it to kill the thirsting of his system for nicotine.

THREE

'It won't bloody do, you know,' McKeown shouted down the phone. 'It just won't bloody do! We know Hitler was a difficult man to deal with, for God's sake! Kinnell!... We were fighting the bastard for six years! We don't want to know what pills he gave him; we don't want to know that he saved his sodding life! We want some personal stuff, some colour, and how Morell got out of Germany. Now get back there and get some stuff we can read! I want more out of a day's interviewing than the fact that the Führer was a sweaty heavy farter! So get on with it. By the way,' McKeown subsided, 'are you ready for a panchromatic artiste?'

'Not yet. A photographer wouldn't help.' replied Ritter, unperturbed by the outburst. 'They're talking OK. I only told you all that to show that they're opening up in detail. In fact it is all good stuff – Himmler setting up a mass murderer to try and kill Speer, all that. It'll all gel together in the end. The trouble is that Morell doesn't remember things in chronological order, and he doesn't even remember some things he told me maybe a few hours earlier, and I have to work back through my notes to remind him. It's heavy going, but it's coming along, well enough.'

'Fair enough,' McKeown conceded. 'Are you all right for cash?'

'I am for the time being. I'm booked in to a pub across the road, and that's only a few bob a night. I don't know the number, sorry, I'll let you have it next time I ring.'

'Kinnell,' said McKeown, 'I think that's the first time a man on the road's ever refused the offer of money being wired. Are you sure this story hasn't gone to your brain?'

His check call completed, Ritter strolled around the village. It didn't take long: one street, with cul-de-sacs off,

one church, one pub, one general store, one bus stop on either
side of the street, about two hundred houses clustered around
a heathery hilltop, divided into fields by walls that were
actually merely piles of stones. All that, and one escaper from
the Berlin bunker to whose life story Ritter reapplied himself.

*The Führer would arrive on our doorstep out of the sky
without any warning. He'd just come round on Sunday
teatime and if it was nice weather we'd all sit in the garden,
otherwise we would sit beside the fire.*

'Well,' suggested Ritter, 'if he'd bought the house,
perhaps he felt entitled – did he buy you the house, as he'd
promised, for curing his eczema?'

'Not exactly. I suppose he knew we must already have
had a house in Berlin, so he really meant he would buy me a
villa in Obersalzburg. But we already had a villa on the Baltic
coast at Heringsdorf and we wanted to move anyway, and we
bought a new house in Berlin, in Inselstrasse, in
Schwanenwerder. It was very expensive, more than 300,000
Reichsmarks, and the Führer gave me first a loan of 200,000
Reichsmarks, and then made it a gift. I paid the rest myself.'

'Inselstrasse?' repeated Ritter: 'the one on Pfaueninsel?
Peacock Island? Very smart.'

'He called it The Bakehouse,' interjected Mrs Morell,
'and he called me his pastry cook, because I baked almond
cakes, just the way he liked them. And he would come and
ask for cakes. He even sent word for me to send cakes to him
when he was in France. Once I gave him cheese for tea and
when he realised later that cheese was rationed he sent a man
round with the coupons. He was generous in little ways like
that.'

Between them, the Morells talked at length about the
generosity, the personality, and the sense of humour of Adolf
Hitler.

'Humour? Tell me one of his jokes,' said Ritter.

It wasn't like jokes, but it was funny. He had this shaky arm, you know, and he said once that it was a good thing it was his arm that was shaking and not his head all the time – otherwise it would be bad news for everybody! And he did impersonations. He did Mussolini, and most of the people in the bunker…

And they talked of his ambitions. Hitler had planned to retire early, it seemed, and to live in Linz, which was virtually the same altitude as his birthplace, Braunau, on the Inn river, 'and the Führer also said that man works better at the altitude at which he was born'. On they went until Ritter thought that he had more than enough 'colour' to satisfy even McKeown.

'Tell me,' he said, 'about the bunker.'

It was not a healthy place to live and work. It was fifty feet underground and early in 1939 it flooded when some sewers broke in a really heavy downpour and the walls and floors and the new carpet – it was around the time the Chancellery opened – were stained with filth. Some of the priceless works of art were ruined. And living inside was atrocious; you only breathed re-circulated air – it would have been no good for a sufferer from migraine, no good at all – and the whine of the air conditioning went on all day and night. The entire place was unhealthy; I had to have a special vegetable garden constructed that used only filtered water and pure fertilizers in an attempt to get some clean living into the system. And to be frank, most of the people in the bunker were not very nice people, either.

Wonderful! thought Ritter. McKeown is going to love that observation!

Most of them were younger than me; I was 53 at the beginning of the war. And most of them were in the SS.

Brandt was an army lieutenant colonel – don't ask me how. So I was really the only one without a uniform. Because it made security easier, I got the Führer's permission to wear a uniform, so long as it wasn't an official outfit, and I got his own tailor to make me up two uniforms, one in brown and one in grey, with a bit of gold braid so that they looked official. The SS hated that, and insisted that I didn't wear an SS badge on the belt buckle, that's how small-minded everybody was. As if I would have wanted to wear an SS badge!

They were also jealous because I had my own rooms – a bedroom and a drawing room – inside the Führer's private quarters. It was exactly opposite his anteroom and study, across the conference passage. Nobody else was that close. I was on very good terms with the secretaries and stenographers, and people like the pilots, but the SS resented my close relationship with the Führer. Even Hoffmann resented me, later. Bormann and I got on well, but the others left me out of everything, even if they were going out together for an evening. And that in spite of the fact that every one of them was treated medically by me at some time or another.

It didn't make things better when the Führer said to them that apart from Eva Braun and his dog Blondi, Bormann and I were the only ones he could trust. Imagine how jealous they all were! None of that worried me though; I was too busy. While they were organising their little conspiracies I was busy setting up pharmacies and research laboratories to produce more medicine for the Reich.

Ritter knew about that 'patriotic' work, from Bayer's research. In common with many doctors of the period, Morell had 'kick-back' deals with different pharmacies to which he sent prescriptions, producing an average twenty per cent of the medicine costs. Before the war he had been part-owner of a Hamburg pharmaceutical company, which he took over completely during the war. He was a member of the board of a firm making the emulsion that settled Hitler's stomach, and of another that made the anti-cold treatment – it was a treatment not available in Germany; Morell had a large shareholding in the firm that made the tablets, in Budapest. His position as physician to Hitler's 'court' enabled him to build factories as well as to patent remedies. He became sole supplier of vitamin chocolates for the troops, and his 'Russia Brand' lice-powder was made compulsory throughout the armed forces.

Ritter questioned the financial advantage of Morell's position.

You should realise that this was not abnormal. Hoffmann was the only person allowed to photograph the Führer, and the copyright of all the photographs remained his, even after the war. At the same time, I was receiving nothing, don't forget, from my practice on Kurfurstendamm. Just as Hoffmann was receiving no normal income from his studio. And of course the Führer knew all about it. Some people complained about it, but my researches were all proved to be worthwhile when I eventually discovered penicillin.

'You...? You discovered... penicillin?' Ritter managed to suppress a smile: 'It's the first I've heard of it.'

'Well, it's true. I spent years working on it, mostly on my own. I put in a lot of work and of course a lot of my own money. I even used it on patients in the Chancellery, but before I could do anything about it, the entire work was stolen by the British Secret Service and the credit went to some obscure English researcher.'

While it was clear to Ritter that he was confronting a total fantasist, he felt that he was growing to sympathise with the man, without actually liking him, although the doctor seemed desperate to be liked.

Towards the end, the Führer was a wreck. Not physically, I made sure of that, although the pressures of day-to-day events were quite clearly taking their toll. The usual physical sign of mental stress was throbbing headache or tremor in his left arm and left leg, both things I could deal with. Oddly, this tremor disappeared for some time after the assassination attempt. The Führer had been used to pressing his left hand against his breast, or holding it with his right hand, to control the tremors. But after the explosion it stopped shaking completely.

You know, the whole thing, the episode of the Attentat – *the assassination attempt – on the Führer, was a miracle! Nobody could believe that it was anything but the intervention of Providence that saved the Führer's life.*

It was just before one in the afternoon on July 20, 1944, at the Wolf's Lair, Rastenberg, and there was this big crash. I was convinced that the Allies had found us and were bombing us. Then Heinz Linge, Hitler's valet, came rushing in and said: 'Quick, Herr Professor! You must come to the Führer at once!'

I ran to the place, it was a barrack hut, and everything was full of smoke and there were splinters of wood and glass everywhere. You know Colonel Count von Stauffenberg had put a briefcase with a timebomb under the map table. It was against the feet of Heinrich Berger, a shorthand writer: he had to go to hospital, poor chap, and von Hasselbach amputated both legs. But the Führer was already in his own quarters when I arrived. He was dazed, but I think more by the incredulity that he had survived, than by the pain, which must have been immense – I took more than a hundred wood splinters from his legs, they were oak from the table he'd been leaning on. But he looked at me and said: 'It's nothing, really!'

Then he laughed: 'I'm immortal! I'm invulnerable! I'm invincible!' His hair was badly singed – it had been on fire – and his right arm was bruised and temporarily paralysed. Although he was wearing a bullet-proof vest, his back had been lacerated by flying glass. His uniform was burned and shredded, his trouser legs had actually been blown off, but he was only concerned with changing into fresh clothes so that he could go and meet Mussolini, who was arriving that afternoon. While I was preparing bandages for his wounds, he was telling me to hurry up! In fact, the blast had damaged his eardrums slightly. Apart from that, well, the Führer had to greet Mussolini by shaking his hand with his left hand. Otherwise no ill effects. Everyone else was also assured that the Führer was truly invincible, and immortal.

It wasn't, after all, the first attempt on his life that he had survived. An Englishman tried to shoot him in the very early days – there's even an English novel written about that. In November 1939 a bomb blew up the Burgerbraukeller in Munich ten minutes after the Führer had left to get his train to Nuremberg; it killed eight party comrades and seriously injured another sixty. Again, there were two Englishmen behind that, and they were caught and tried and sent to Dachau. Then once at the Berghof someone sent a gift of a dog that turned out to have rabies, and once some cherries were delivered that were poisoned. The Führer introduced food tasters after that. But he survived everything!

For years we in Berlin had been largely unaffected by the war: rationing came late to us, we never seemed short of the essentials. He had made sure of that. But we started to hear the bombs falling. And of course eventually we came to feel them in the capital itself.

'And then by the last Christmas,' said Ritter, 'in 1944, people were saying: "Be practical this year – give a coffin!"...' But Morell ignored him.

At the beginning of April Hitler at last realised that Berlin was not invulnerable, as he had always claimed. The main daily war conference was moved below ground to the bunker, and he started to move non-essential staff out of Berlin to safety.

By the end of the first week in April the basic drugs I needed were in short supply, or impossible to get, even for the Führer. The Engels pharmacy, on which I had relied, ran out of medicines. Only one chemist still had supplies. I remember that the SS main office, which was supposed to be maintaining basic drugs, also ran out.

At the end of the third week – literally on Saturday April 21 – it was the chaos time. The Russian artillery had just moved up within range, and shells were raining down on all the main buildings. There was an almost permanent air raid alert. The Russians were shelling all the main government buildings. The generals had got to Bormann and convinced him that one way or another, the Führer had to be got out of Berlin and out to the south, even if it meant that he was smuggled out against his will, because he was saying things like he wanted to die in the capital. And even that he wanted a Viking funeral, his corpse to be burned with his dog at his feet, like in an opera.

But because he was invincible, he said, he would forced to do what his enemies could not: he had to take his own life! When Bormann told me about this, saying that we had to stop him, I was appalled at the suggestion that we should conspire against the Führer, even on this subject. But the future of the Reich was synonymous with the life of the Führer. Eventually Bormann and the generals convinced me that, as a loyal servant and a loyal German, I had no choice but to exercise my professional expertise and knowledge while the superior knowledge of my Führer was temporarily impaired.

That Saturday night I went as though to give him his usual glucose shot. But he grabbed my wrist, the one holding the hypodermic, and he screamed at me: 'Do you think I'm crazy? I know what's in that needle. It's not glucose, it's morphine!'

So I made sure he watched while I squirted the liquid out of the cylinder, then showed him a glucose phial and drew the liquid from it into the hypodermic. This time he allowed me to inject him. But I had switched the liquids in advance.

While it was taking effect, he held my shoulders and said: 'You must get away from here, Morell. Get out of that uniform, into your ordinary clothes and go back to being the doctor on the Kurfurstendamm! You must act as if you've never seen me. If you are asked, say you never even knew me!'

You see: even at what he thought was the end of his life he was showing that he cared for me, and for my wife. He was grateful for all the good works I had done for him. He wasn't aware of it, but all order had already broken down inside the bunker. The SS were bringing in young girls, ostensibly for their safety, and they were openly having sex in all the offices. There were naked women, offering themselves to anybody, everywhere in the bunker...

A few minutes after the injection he collapsed in his chair. The generals had cleared the staircase entrances and removed the guards. Between us we carried him up to a car with curtains at the windows and drove out of the Chancellery garages into Hermann Goering Strasse. It wasn't easy. We got through the Brandenburg Gate, up the Chalottenburger Chaussee, to the Tiergarten railway station, then Masuren Allee to the Hitler Youth headquarters.

Morell was gazing at the ceiling, picturing the escape route in his mind.

From there we went along Reichsstrasse to the Reichssportfeld and over Heerstrasse and down to the bridgehead at Pichelsdorf at the north end of the Havel. That was as far as we could get by road.

There were some boats and we sailed down the lake – at one time we were not very far from my home on Peacock Island – as far as Gatow aerodrome. It was after midnight when we took off in one of the Führer's Focke-Wulf Kondor courier planes, the big four-engined ones. Hanna Reich, the air ace, the only person Bormann would trust to fly the Führer, was the pilot. Ours was the last flight out of Berlin. I remember that we actually flew over the Russian lines at Juterborg and then above burning villages and across the American lines at Partenkirchen. We were zigzagging all over the country looking for the field. And then through the searchlights and anti-aircraft fire until we eventually found the airfield at Neubiberg. After that, things became a bit chaotic. I managed to make sure that the Führer was in safe hands, but then I had slight heart attack myself – even doctors are not immune from such excitements and anxieties and in fact my heart had been bad for nearly two years – and I found myself first in a clinic and then in the city hospital in Bad Reichenhall.

I was still there on May 18 when General Patton's soldiers, as part of a sweep for SS officers who were hiding like cowards in hospitals, found me there and I was arrested.

'Arrested? And they let you go?'

I wasn't an SS man. I wasn't a war criminal. And even war criminals were released. You must understand that conditions were absolutely chaotic in the summer of 1945. And there was confusion because the English and French were often asking for specific German officers. Eisenhower had given orders for the most severe treatment of the Nazis, and all SS men were automatically war criminals, but General Patton ignored this to a large extent. He even sent home some SS men after they had been arrested and interviewed, hundreds of them. They just went home from Bavaria and showed their release papers to the soldiers who had arrested them. That is the real reason, I expect, that Patton was sacked, not as they said that he had been dining with a few Nazis. Some of them finished up working for western intelligence, even.

Most of the real war criminals were got out by your Secret Service, what you now call MI6. They did this because there were German Nazis, distantly related to your British royal family, the Hesse family and Mountbatten, who should have been dealt with for war crimes. It was important to avoid embarrassment that they never got to court, and also that the people associated with them were not charged, either. Most SS people passed through British or French hands, and lots of them were offered jobs working against the Communists, or sent out via an organisation called Odessa. Odessa worked through British prison camps in Bavaria, Northern Italy, and Yugoslavia. There was another organisation, called Spinne – spider – they were both organised by MI6.

At the end of 1944 we had become aware that some senior officers were planning to get out of Germany. They collected personal possessions and some loot and paintings, and moved their cars up to the border and sometimes exchanged them for French or American cars. My bank manager told me that officers were transferring money into Spanish bank accounts.

Mrs Morell interrupted the flow: 'We moved some furniture, and some carpets and paintings, out to Bad Reichenhall.'

'Not out of the country, like the others. Only beyond the range of the bombers,' her husband quickly corrected.

The escape organisation was all rather informal, I think. It was a way of escape, rather than a means of keeping the Nazi party alive, as some people believe now. There was a common interest among the people who were involved, and they helped each other with things like routes, places to hide, what they called safe houses, and guides, and forged papers. But it wasn't properly organised until the British took it over. They operated it from the camps as far as Genoa, on one route, and Rome on another. I think another way they ran it was into Portugal. They called these escape routes 'rat-lines', as if they disapproved – but they were in charge of them.

I had always intended to go back to Berlin; I wasn't on any wanted list. Then I learned that the Russians wanted me to help identify a body – the body. That would have meant a Soviet prison camp for me, so I too took the so-called rat-line, to Rome. I stayed a few weeks in a Franciscan convent on via Sicilia, just off the Via Veneto, and then they gave me an Italian Red Cross passport...

Morell pulled out a drawer beneath the table, opened an old tobacco tin and produced the document.

...Number 101080, which said I was a doctor born in Bologna, and I made my way here. We'd actually earmarked the place earlier. My English was good enough, and Ireland was well disposed towards Germany, just as the Vatican was – Mr de Valera, you probably know, had sent his condolences after the news of the Führer's death.

Ritter had been biting his tongue for some time. 'Just a minute!' he interjected. 'But... Hold on, let's go back a bit. Are you saying... do you mean... you did say, didn't you...' He was rapidly flicking back through the pages of his notebook... 'But Hitler didn't die, did he...? He wasn't, er... wasn't burned and buried outside the bunker, was he? You told me you'd got him out...!'

It was a mistake. Morell had been in full flow when Ritter interrupted him. He had now stopped and was trying to concentrate on what he was saying, or wanted to say, and to remember what he had actually said. He sighed.

'Did I say that? Are you sure? I suppose I did, then. So I suppose it follows, doesn't it, that if his was not the body buried outside the bunker he must have been buried somewhere else?'

'But where was he buried?'

'I can think of a million reasons why I should not tell you that.'

'Six million, even. But you said the Russians wanted you to identify the body. You said "the body".'

'I know I did. But it wasn't Hitler's body. It was something they had arranged in the bunker after we had left.'

'You're gonna have to tell me. You realise that.'

But, at least for the time being, the doctor had clammed up.

FOUR

McKeown had told him to come down to his home for lunch
on Sunday. Both men had agreed that as the story progressed
it was better not to use the phone to discuss details, and Ritter
also now had serious problems about what he was going to
write.

On Saturday night he'd had dinner with his best friends,
Roger and Barbara Stewart. They were both journalists on
rival newspapers, but journalists Ritter knew he could trust
totally: they'd be embarrassed if their own editor ever
discovered they knew another paper's secrets – but not as
embarrassed as they would in betraying a friend. So Ritter
told them the story.

'It's a great tale,' said Roger. 'But you've got to find the
real grave. That's all there is to it. You've got to make him
tell you. Then you've cracked it. The story about MI5 or 6 is
good, but nothing's as good as Hitler's real grave. It's like
the One True Cross.'

'You can see Morell's problem,' said Barbara. 'Wherever
it is, people will desecrate it. The fascists will want to rob it
for the bones so they have relics of their leader or even as the
basis of a new party. You know, like in that movie. The Jews
will want to destroy it to prevent anything like that
happening. Either way, it will have to be dug up so that the
government can confirm or deny the story, and so the Nazis
and the Israelis can't bugger about with the bits. Come to
that, the Russians are going to be none-too-pleased with him,
either. They claim to have the real body.'

She thought for a moment. '…What are you going to have
– a photo of a grave…? With or without a headstone…? Did
he say if it has a headstone…? Do you know…? Do you have
any clues at all…? I'll bet it doesn't have a cross – although,

if it's in a Catholic cemetery... Is it a proper grave, though...?
Is it in a cemetery, or what?'

'I don't know. I don't know any details about the grave at
all. He just won't talk about it. I can't say I blame him, when
I think about it,' said Ritter.

'Anyway, look on the bright side,' said Roger, reaching
into his cupboard for a fresh bottle of wine, 'At least you've
got a book to write. You know, life in the bunker, the flight
from Berlin, British intelligence, Hitler's actual death... the
couple living in fear of discovery for all those years... you
can pad it out a bit, with them counting the time, listening to
the ticking of the clock on the mantlepiece... wondering
whether one day somebody like you will come along to
wreck their wretched lives...'

'They haven't got a clock on the mantlepiece.'

'Don't be pedantic: the ticking of the clock, wherever it
is.'

'You know, I don't think they have a clock at all.'

'Silly sod! Everybody has a clock. How else do they know
when the *Forsyte Saga* or Alf Garnett is on?'

'They certainly haven't got a telly,' said Ritter.

'Well *Mrs Dale's Diary* then!' laughed Roger. 'People
have a clock to know what time their programmes are on the
radio, or what time to have lunch. And if they haven't got a
clock, they have a watch, so it's the same thing. Watching the
seconds tick by.'

Ritter brought to his mind's eye the picture of Morell
taking his pulse. 'Bloody hell! Do you know, he took my
pulse, but he wasn't wearing a watch!'

'Watches, clocks, it's all academic,' said Barbara, putting
a bowl of salad on the dining table. 'Let's eat.'

'It's not academic,' protested Roger. 'Not if you're
watching the seconds tick by. There's got to be a clock
somewhere.'

'Well I don't need a clock to tell you it's time for dinner, that your dinner's on the table, and that it you don't eat it, husband mine, Ritter surely will.'

*

McKeown lived in an old mill house in Kent. It straddled a millstream and the mill wheel still turned inside the house. But, as the news editor persistently complained when showing visitors round, it did not produce even enough power to heat his water. It was a listed building, massive, and set in five acres that McKeown's flower power sons had given over to donkeys and hens. They had one hen called Albert: Albert Our Hen. It was McKeown's joke, a pun on the wartime prison escape film, *Albert RN.*

Like the Stewarts, McKeown was adamant that the best story was the identification of the actual grave.

'Intelligence will shit themselves about the rat-line,' he said, sucking on his glasses. 'But that's the follow-up. One way or another he's got to tell you where the grave is. That's all that matters. People will desecrate it. The fascists will dig it up, and the Jews will want it destroyed. The Russians will want it destroyed more than anybody. They'll look real silly buggers for pretending they've had his body all this time. But none of that will happen: we'll dig it up.'

'We can't go round digging up bloody graves!' Ritter protested.

'...At least, we'll get the authorities to open the grave. We'll make a deal: nobody does anything about the story until the body's up and checked, then we have the first crack at it, the story all ready to go, exclusively, with the full forensic report: *Post* Finds Hitler. And while everybody's chasing his tail, we'll follow up with all the background. Kinnell, Tex, it's a cracker!'

'How can we get a body exhumed on the quiet?'

'When you're dealing with a thing like this you can get anything done on the quiet. It needs one of the authorities – MI6, MI5, the Special Branch, anybody we decide to take into our confidence, anybody we decide to give the credit to, especially anybody who wants to score points off some other bunch of sad bastards – and they'll bring in a tame JP to sign an exhumation order, then they'll seal off the area, no problem. And in return they'll go along with more or less any deal we want. You'll be famous, my son!'

'Famous, if I can get him to talk.'

McKeown doled out great spoonfuls of made-from-a-packet paella – the food favoured by non-cooks whenever their wives were away – onto two earthenware plates. 'I think you're going to have to tell him that you'll rat on the deal about his confidentiality, that you'll tell people where he is.'

'The Israelis will kidnap him. They'll put him on trial in Tel Aviv.'

'You don't actually have to do it. Anyway, the Israelis don't want him. He's not a war criminal.'

'Oh? How do you know? I mean, that's what he says, and what I think is possibly true. But how do you know?'

'Jake looked him up.'

'Sodding hell! You've told Jake? You told me not even to speak to Donald.'

'Yes, I know, but you've got to let me handle things the way I think best.'

'But Jake's Jewish, for God's sake! Where do you think he looked Morell up? Who told him Morell wasn't a war criminal? – The Wiener library? The Jewish Documentation Centre? Simon Wiesenthall's office? The embassy in Kensington Palace Green?'

'Jake's Jewish but he's the managing editor of the *Post*, first. Would you not have told me about the Vatican connection if I'd been Catholic? How do you think these stories ever get in the paper if you don't tell anybody?'

'The editor's a Catholic. I suppose he'll be OK about the Vatican stuff?'

'It's not exactly world shattering, is it, that the Pope was trying to be ambidextrous, supporting both sides? There was a hell of a row when he blessed the fascist troops during the war. Anyway, what do you think about this paella – it only needs one pan, and a fork, in fact you can eat it out of the pan, Spanish style, then there's hardly any washing up.'

Ritter's mind wasn't on the meal. 'It's OK, thanks. I'd just rather you hadn't told anybody yet, that's all.'

'You can trust Jake with your life, Tex. My word on that.'

'It's not that. You know it's not. It's just that keeping secrets is not part of a newspaperman's culture. His job is spilling secrets. That's the problem.'

*

'Ritter's pissed off with me for telling you about Morell,' said McKeown.

'Bugger me, cock! Who does the lanky bastard think he is?'

'It's not like that. I let drop that I knew Morell wasn't a war criminal and he was vexed that you knew about it and had checked up.'

'Just because he's got a big story, he's playing the primadonna is he?'

'No. But, while he's out of order in one way, he's worried about the security of the job. After all, it is his story. He brought it in himself. Where did you actually check it out?'

'Look,' said Morris. 'It isn't his story. It is our story. It's the *Post*'s story. It's a long time since I was a reporter, since I actually crunched up the gravel path, I know. But he's not the only bastard with contacts. We all keep our good contacts. I just dropped the Morell name on one of mine and he knew instantly that he had been cleared after the war.'

'What? An embassy contact?'

'Don't you bloody start! A contact, that's all. An old pal. Anyway, how's he getting on with it?'

'Oh it's coming along pretty well,' said McKeown. 'Developing more or less as it should.'

'Anything new?'

'Not really. Just the sort of things we expected.'

*

The Sunday night ferry crossing to Dun Laoghaire was spoiled for Ritter by a violent thunder storm, a group of drunken teenagers singing Procul Harem's A *Whiter Shade Of Pale* to the accompaniment of an accordion, and the fact that the lighting was too dim for him to start reading *In Cold Blood*, by Truman Capote.

The morning was overcast, and threatening rain, but two playings of *Paperback Writer*, a Beatles' number one record, on his car radio, cheered him up: he had been the first person to hear the lyrics of that song and soon, he'd probably be a paperback writer, even a hardback writer, himself.

He parked the Rapier outside the Morells' house, rapped on the door, and was invited in by Mrs Morell, who said she would put the kettle on.

*

'Ted? It's McKeown. It occurred to me that somewhere in your organisation you must have a Hitler expert. I wondered if you might bring him along and have a spot of lunch, tomorrow.'

'Hitler expert? Why would we want a Hitler expert?'

'You know, the bunker, the SS, the war criminals, that sort of thing.'

'Not us, Bill. Not Hitler experts. Complete dicks, us, nothing sawn off. Try the kosher nostril.'

'But you must have somebody who's an expert on the bunker, and what happened after the end.'

'Well, you were there, and I was. But that doesn't make either of us experts. Of course, there's Trevor-Roper, or Blenkinsop, if you need that level of expertise. But, best thing is if you buy me lunch, and we sort it out from there.'

*

'Better watch the *Post* over the next few days,' Roger Stewart confided to Vincent Mulchrone, the *Daily Mail*'s chief feature writer, in the back bar of the Harrow pub. 'I hear that Ritter's got himself a world-beater.'

'Good for Tex.' He nodded to the landlord, his signal to open another half-bottle of Moet. 'And how is young Mr Ritter, these days?'

'With this story, he's like a dog with two dicks.'

'He would be,' said Mulchrone, sagely. 'Journalism is the only form of human activity where the orgasm comes at the beginning.'

*

McKeown was standing at the basement bar in Simpson's-in-the-Strand with a pewter tankard full of draught Bass in readiness for his old colleague's arrival. They shook hands and walked immediately to a corner banquette to talk privately.

'You understand,' said McKeown, 'that this is strictly between the two of us. At this stage I just want your advice, but it mustn't go any further.'

'Not a word.'

'The point is... Well, the point is that it looks to us as if Adolf and Eva – well, I'm not totally sure about Eva, but Adolf, anyway – didn't die in the bunker. That their remains weren't burned in the Chancellery grounds. In other words, that the body the Russians have isn't Hitler at all.'

'Where do you get all this fairytale stuff?'

'One of my reporters has found Hitler's doctor, Morell. He was also supposed to be dead, but he isn't. We've established that he's alive and well, and he's talking. He's not telling everything, but the lad's still working on him.'

'Have you seen this doctor?'

'Of course not.'

'Well, I reckon he's lying, don't you?'

'Who – the doctor or Ritter?'

'One or the other. It's preposterous, isn't it? There were witnesses to the suicide, witnesses to the burning, there's even a will. What's he like, this Ritter? A drinker? On LSD, is he? Is he a loony?'

'Come on, Ted, he's a proper reporter. Been with me since he came out.'

'What was he in?'

'The Fighting Fifth. But, the point is this: OK, as I tell it to you, with no proof on the table, you don't believe it. What if it's true?'

'Seriously, Bill, you can't expect me to believe this rubbish. Where is he supposed to be, this doctor?'

'I don't want to tell you that yet. What I want to know is, what would you do?'

The two men moved up to the ground floor to discuss the problem over the roast beef.

'Let's assume for the moment,' said McKeown, holding his house claret up to the light, 'that everything I've told you is true, that Hitler wasn't burned then buried in Berlin but somewhere else, and that we can prove it.'

'And nobody knows except the *Post*? You'd have a scoop and we'd have to put security tightly round it, wherever it is. Starting with this doctor. Is he in England? We'd have to interview him, that goes without saying. We might get

Trevor-Roper to do that, I suppose. He'd have been down to do it last time. Where is this doctor?'

'He's not a million miles away, wherever he is.'

'Have you "brought him up", to use what I believe to be the Fleet Street vernacular?'

'Bought him up... We haven't spent a penny on him, nor promised one. Nor do we expect to.'

McKeown watched as the headwaiter crossed the floor, whispered to the diner with an open-necked shirt sitting at another table, and handed him a necktie. The waiter then walked over to McKeown, and said: 'Terribly sorry, sir, I don't know how that happened; he's an American.'

The two friends laughed. 'Be letting bloody women in next,' said Ted. 'Look, if it's true – and I honestly don't believe it – you can see what the problems would be. We'd have to seal the grave off, wherever it is – let's trust it's in western Europe since you say so coyly that he ain't a million miles away – and we'd have to dig it up, to see what we've got. We'd have to be pretty dead certain before we'd even go to that stage, and you'd have to be a hundred per cent before you published anything. In fact, logic demands that you would do nothing at all until you had the forensic proof, one way or another. And you'd have to rely on us for that.'

McKeown said he would agree to that.

'In return, obviously, we'd go along with what you wanted, within reason, to preserve your exclusivity. But look, we're talking as if this is true, which it isn't, because the Russians have him.' He paused. '...And we're ignoring the fact that they have Graham's port on the list. In Ireland before the war – you of all people must know that most port importers are Irish – when there was a ball at a country house they used to allow three bottles of port per man, and one bottle per woman... Ah, there you are,' he said to a waiter; 'Two large Grahams, please.'

'In the days you're talking about,' said McKeown, 'the stuff wasn't fortified. Three bottles now would be a lethal dose. There are still people in Scotland who won't touch it because the English forced them to switch from claret to port when France fell out of favour.' He swilled the drink round in his glass, sniffed it, and quoted:

'Firm and erect the Highland chieftain stood. Old was his mutton, and his claret good. "Thou shalt drink port", the English statesman cried. He drank the poison, and his spirit died...'

'...Hell, you Hibernians never knew what was good for you.' He examined his glass, drank the wine and turned back to McKeown: 'Now, this doctor, Morell? You say he's supposed to be dead. Why isn't he?'

'He got out of the bunker, he says, with Hitler, just before the end, and they flew to Munich. Morell was captured and released and came out through the ratline, via Rome. We don't know where Adolf died, maybe Munich – Morell had a heart attack somewhere near there, was arrested, and released – the Tyrol, somewhere. Maybe he's in the old Hitler family plot, for all I know. We're still trying to get that out of him.'

'Leave it with me. Let me dwell on it overnight.'

'Yes, of course, Ted. But meanwhile, not a word to anyone about the story, please.'

'Not a word. You know me: silent as the... er, grave.'

*

'Get me everything you have on Ritter, Charles, reporter on the *Post*, national service in the Northumberland Fusiliers. And find out what sort of car he drives. And if he takes it out of the country.'

*

As Jake Morris waited to be admitted to the *Post* car park, the security man asked him: 'Excuse me, Mr Morris, that blue

Sunbeam we sometimes have in the car park: belongs to Mr Ritter, doesn't it?'

'That's right, why do you ask?'

'No reason. Just hadn't seen him about for a while. Abroad is he?'

'I don't think so. I expect he's just on an out of town job.'

*

When Morris got home he rang the contact he had retained from his reporting days 'Dan? Jake here. Somebody's asking questions about the reporter on that special assignment I told you about. I think we should have a meet.'

*

Next morning, in the grey offices of British Intelligence, a young man dropped a manila folder on his boss's desk.

'Right, sir, here we are. There's plenty of dope on your Mr Ritter, and on his car, too. Are you going to tell me why you want all this?'

'Not yet. Need to know basis.'

'Suit yourself. Anyway we struck lucky, the *Post*'s security man used to be a Ministry of Defence policeman, a Mod plod, who took his pension and went out to civvie street. The car's a two-tone blue Sunbeam Rapier, 5301 PT. The runners of the driver's seat have been moved back two inches to provide more legroom; the ashtray's been replaced by a larger one, possibly from a Humber. The back seat's usually covered in old faded newspapers and empty Rothman's packets, you know what scruffy buggers these Fleet Street types are. The front bonnet is pitted by shit and dead flies as if it's been used for hill-climbs. There's a GB plate on the back, but we don't know where the car is at the moment. We're working on that.'

'Good enough. And the lad himself?'

'Born 1938, 29 now. Five GCEs including French and German. Worked on the *Newcastle Evening Chronicle*, opted on call-up for the Northumberlands, local lot, turned down Int and the Service Corps – he also had shorthand and typing – and then turned down the chance of a commission on the grounds that he couldn't afford officers' mess bills. Got two stripes up as assistant to the CO and the Int Officer; the battalion was in Munster, most of the time. His German is fluent, apparently. Excellent conduct. Nothing against him. He's six-two, dark brown hair, blue-grey eyes, twelve stone: on the lean side. No diseases, no distinguishing marks. One interesting thing. Apparently he suffers from some sort of debilitating migraine. He didn't declare it until he was in. If he had, he could have got out of call-up on medical grounds. So he obviously actually wanted to join up.'

'Why would he do that? Do you know about his politics?'

'Not really. The *Post*'s a Tory paper, though.'

'That means nothing. Most of the Commies in Fleet Street are on the *Telegraph* or the *Financial Times*. The Tories are all on the *Mirror* and the *Herald*.'

He smiled at his assistant to show that he was not really complaining. 'Look, what else have you got?'

'As a reporter he covered some fairly big stories last year, according to the *Post* cuttings. He was in Viet Nam; he did some work on the moors murders, and on the Kray twins. He did the George Blake escape and he was sent to cover the Aberfan disaster.'

'Where's he live?'

'In a basement flat in Marloes Road, you know: off Cromwell Road, near the air terminal, it's where, er…'

'The Devonshire pub; good sausages.'

'I was going to say St Mary Abbots Hospital, but yes, the sausages are good at the Devonshire.'

'He shares the place with another reporter, a Scotsman.'

'Good God! He's not a shirt lifter, is he?'

'No, he's married all right. But his wife lives in Northumberland. I think it's what they probably call a modern marriage; apparently Ritter sometimes does a favour for the news editor's secretary. That's a woman. Well, a girl, really.'

'Get somebody to check that he's not at the secretary's place, and not at his wife's, will you? And what does the Fleet Street scuttlebutt say he's up to now?'

'They don't know. Apparently he's on what they call a "news editor's special".'

The assistant pulled a piece of flimsy paper from a file. 'I saved the best to last. There's one other little thing, which may or may not be relevant. His father was killed at Dunkirk. In rather interesting circumstances, I'd say.'

He slid the paper across the desk: 'I wonder whether the *Post* knows it employs the son of a decorated war hero?'

'Well, what those particular bastards would call a war hero,' said Ted, reading.

FIVE

June 1, 1967

Not many people had the number of the private phone on the desk of Richard Helms, director of the CIA. But he recognised the voice that said: 'Dick, I have to see you. Now. I'm at the airport. At Dulles. Nobody knows I'm here, I just flew in.' Helms told the caller to take a cab to the CIA headquarters at Langley.

Helms and Meir Amit had been friends when students together at Columbia University. While the American progressed to the top of his country's intelligence-gathering service, Amit rose to the top of Israel's – Mossad. Now, protected by air-conditioning from the heavy heat of a Virginian summer, he was seeking tacit approval for a pre-emptive strike by Israel against Egypt and Syria.

Amit talked all day with Helms and his Middle East experts. At six o'clock he had convinced them that his case should be put to Defense Secretary Robert McNamara, who was called and invited to join them. Halfway through this top-level interview an aide brought an urgent message to the politician. It said that Moshe Dayan had just been appointed Minister of Defense for Israel.

McNamara handed the telex to Amit. 'Tell Moshe,' he said, 'that whatever decision he takes, I wish him good luck.'

The men shook hands and as McNamara left the office the Israeli turned to his old college pal.

'Tell me what you know about Hitler's bones.'

Even before the war was over, Amit explained to an astonished Helms, the Jewish Brigade of the British Army had organised a special squad whose sole purpose was to track down Nazis. They called themselves *Hanokmin*, after a

Biblical reference to the avenging angels of God. Most of the people they traced were the SS men who had organised and run the concentration camps.

'To begin with we handed them over to the Allied military authorities. But they frequently escaped in the chaos that inevitably followed the end of hostilities. And some were simply allowed to walk free. Not surprisingly, some elements of *Hanokmin* took the law into their own hands. In their official British khaki they would arrest the Nazis – but then take them to a quiet field or wood, read out the crimes and the sentence, and execute the criminals. More than a thousand were dealt with in this way. But the Allies had actually connived with many escapes, even to the extent of listing escapers as dead. One such was Theodor Morell, who was Hitler's personal doctor. He was not a war criminal, as such, but he was never interviewed formally, and now it appears that the official – which is largely Soviet – story of Hitler's so-called death in the bunker is at least dubious. If it is the case that Hitler's body is in other than Soviet hands, we need to find it and to destroy it utterly. One single bone could be the foundation of an entirely new Hitler movement.'

Ed Nelson, the CIA liaison officer with the Justice Department, was listening to the story with a sympathetic ear.

'Half the Nazis running around South America right now were set free by us,' he agreed. 'Some of them we could find immediately. Most have disappeared for ever. Morell was one of those I really thought was dead. If the Brits have found him alive, I'll get Grosvenor Square on to it. It won't take our boys there long to get it out of them.'

'We don't think MI6 has found him, yet,' said Amit; 'They're looking for him.'

'Bet we find him first, in that case,' said Nelson.

*

'They don't take car numbers at the ports any longer, Ted. But it's just possible that the blue Sunbeam you were looking for went either to Dunkirk or Dun Laoghaire.'

'Not much difference, is there? How do you work that out?'

'Well, his last foreign job, if you call it foreign, was in Ireland, and when he went there he went with his car, via Dun Laoghaire. There may be a connection there. But the word on the Street is that he's gone to Dunkirk, although nobody knows for why.'

'Well, we'd better put a man on each port, waiting for the car to come out.'

'This enquiry's to become an operation then, is it? Is it that important?'

'If it's anything at all, it's bloody important. But it might be nothing. We'd better have a full operational meeting before lunch. Oh hell! I've got to meet McKeown today.'

*

Bill McKeown's wife didn't often ring him at the office.

'Can you get one of your people to speak to the GPO about our telephone?' she asked him. 'Half the time it doesn't work, I can't get a line. The rest of the time there's an awful tinny echo.'

'I can hear it,' he told her. 'I'll get someone on to it right away. Look, if Charlie Ritter rings, tell him to ring me on one of the reporters' phones, not on my own phone, will you, love? I always find that if one phone goes wrong, they're all likely to.'

*

'How are things going, Bill? Look, they've got goose on the menu.'

'How do you think, you bastard? You've tapped my home telephone!'

'Hey, come on! Not me, Bill.'

McKeown looked round the bar of the Savile Club to make sure nobody was listening. 'I'm not stupid, you know. What are you hoping to find out?'

'Look, it wasn't me. It is possible that someone in the office might have got a bit enthusiastic, but—'

'But you said you wouldn't tell anybody.'

'That's daft, obviously I had to cover myself in case your flier turned out to be true.'

'We, at my office,' said McKeown, 'have stopped doubting it.'

'You've got to bear in mind that even if he's who he says he is, he's an old man who probably fantasises about his past.'

'And what fantasies,' said McKeown, pulling off his spectacles. 'Especially the parts he tells us about how British intelligence got him out of Germany.'

*

'It's Morell, all right. Absolutely no doubt. The reporter's description ties in with what we have on him, but the truth is that it was our lot who let him out. The Americans arrested him and we asked them to hang on to him, principally so that we had a good excuse to get a look at the Hitler bones. Or what the Reds said were Hitler's bones. When they put out the call for Morell's arrest we said we had no trace of him. Then when the Hitler Youth chap, Axmann, said he'd seen him dead with Bormann, we let that story run, and we got rid of the doctor.'

'In that case, Ted, it means that not only is the Bormann death genuinely doubtful, but that there's a good chance Morell's Hitler story is true.'

'Don't worry about Bormann – if you read the *Express* you see him turning up more frequently than George Best. We've got to concentrate on finding Morell, lifting him from the *Post*, and getting the facts out of him.'

'I'm getting a full team moving on that right now, Ted.'

'Well, find him. Find him before anybody else does.'

*

Outside, in the village street, the air hung heavy and threatening. A recent thunderstorm had failed to clear the air. Indoors it was warm, too. But not that warm. Doctor Morell was nevertheless steaming, literally. Ritter had heard the expression used to describe people in a temper, and he'd probably used it himself. But he'd never actually seen a body steam. He watched the vapour rise from the flabby shoulders, the doctor's shirt once again dark with sweat.

It wasn't fury: it was anxiety, and exasperation. And Ritter was bemused to realise that he noticed the difference in the smell. This time the smell was still ammoniacal, but also sweet, like rotting fruit. Apricots, he decided.

'Haven't I told you enough to make a story for your paper?' he asked. 'Why do you ask me all the time for more? You must see why I cannot tell you what happened to the Führer.'

'It's the Russians, I suppose,' explained Ritter. 'They say they've got Hitler's body. You say they haven't. Or you say what amounts to the fact that they haven't. Look, I'm sorry. If you hadn't told me about it in the first place I wouldn't be asking for more. Likewise, if I hadn't told my boss he wouldn't be asking me to ask you for more. You follow that, don't you? It's not my fault.'

'If I told you that he was buried in a certain grave in a certain place, I know what would happen. People would dig it up.'

'I suppose you're right there, doctor. But, you know, world opinion would probably not go strongly on support for Hitler's right to rest in peace.'

'Well I'm afraid I cannot identify a grave for you.'

The young reporter and the old doctor looked at each other, and then averted their gaze from each other's eyes. It was impasse.

Ritter looked around the room. 'I knew there was something I was going to ask you. Why don't you have a clock in this room? You and Mrs Morell don't even wear watches.'

'We don't need to,' said Morell. 'Look out there…' He pointed his fat finger across the road to Brown's grocery store, opposite. Written on the window in yellowing stick-on letters had once been the words FRY'S CHOCOLATE in a wide white arch, but the capitals R, H and T had long since fallen off. Beneath the arch was a clock, bigger than a mantlepiece clock, with a face more than adequately large to be read from the other side of the street.

'That's taking economy a bit far, isn't it?'

'Not at all. Old people spend most of their lives, you know, sitting watching the world pass by. Mrs Morell and I sit here at this table looking out on the street. Nothing much happens, but we always know what time it is.'

'Have you never had a clock?'

'It doesn't matter. We always know when tea time is.'

As if on cue his wife joined them at the table. She laid down a place mat to protect the plush table cover and put a china teapot on it.

'I've made a special treat for tea,' she said: 'My almond cake.'

*

'Our friends have staffmen in place watching the cars boarding ferries for England from Dunkirk in France and

Dun Laoghaire in Ireland. We are not sure what they are looking for, but they are only interested in blue cars. Ritter has a blue car,' said Ed Nelson.

James Roberts Junior, acting head of the CIA's London station, removed his glasses and pensively cleaned the lenses with a silk handkerchief. 'It's a possibility. It's a remote possibility. But what the hell, we'll get someone to go and watch the watchers watching.'

*

Ritter had been bed-and-breakfasting at the Badgers long enough to be treated almost as a regular at the bar. He'd decided to admit to being a journalist, but to tell people in the village who enquired – as they surely must – that he was on holiday and was toying with writing a book about life in a village such as this. It had the extra advantage that, when he finished talking to the Morells, there were always people ready to join him at the bar with a story offered in possible exchange for a drink. When he wanted company, he stood at the bar. When he wanted solitude, he retired to his room or took himself off for a walk.

There were not many people of his own age; most of the under-thirties had gone off to the towns in search of employment, the notable exception was the girl in the grocer's, a tall girl, young, still in her teens, and with a classical hourglass shape. But he could now recognise villagers at a distance. And also pick out strangers.

The bar of the Badgers was long and narrow and dark, its walls lined by mahogany panels which, somebody said, had once panelled the lounge, or part of the lounge, of a cruise liner. Rusty drawing pins tacked faded grey advertisements, mainly for Guinness, to the panelling. The bar itself was made of Formica, in marbled red. Opposite the bar ran a narrow seat, beneath the window looking out on to the street.

Between the seat and the bar were cast-iron tables with almost certainly the original red marble tops.

Leaning against the bar, and facing the entrance, were two big men, sufficiently similar in their huge, red, cheerful facial characteristics to be related. In spite of the weather they wore green quilted anoraks and flared brown wool trousers. They both ordered Guinness and waited patiently while the landlady reached for glasses and started to fill them slowly.

The man nearest Ritter smiled at him.

'Hot,' he said.

'Very,' said Ritter. 'But the Guinness is cool.' As he spoke, he realised that he was talking like a character in a James Bond novel.

'English?'

Ritter nodded.

'Would you be Mr Ritter?' He nodded again.

The Irishman looked around the bar. 'Would you mind terribly, sir, if we had a quiet word over there, in the corner?'

Ritter shrugged and the two of them went to sit at a table near the door of the Gents. The other Irishman ordered three more pints.

'You don't know me, Mr Ritter. At least, we've never met. But we spoke some time ago on the telephone. Sean Bourke gave you my number.'

'Ah...'

The Irishman put his hand on top of Ritter's, to silence him.

'That's right. Now, what I want to know is why you're still here in Ireland, and what you're doing.'

'Well, nothing, really,' said Ritter. 'Well, I mean, it's just a sort of thing that I'm looking at, something that might turn out to be a story and might not.'

'The Germans, you mean? Are you writing about the Germans?'

For perhaps a whole minute the reporter was nonplussed. He'd worried about his news editor talking to the managing editor. Now it seemed that even the Irish Republican Army was in on the secret. Then suddenly his face cleared and his eyes lit up. He smiled at the Irishman.

'You mean the German farmers? God, no! Nothing to do with the farmers at all, honestly.'

'That's fine, Mr Ritter. However we have a problem. British intelligence has placed a man at Dun Laoghaire docks and he's looking for something. The something he's actually looking for is yourself. Would you believe that, now? Now, what we could do is tell him where you are staying in the likelihood that he'll then depart. You'll have the wit to appreciate of course that if there is one thing we want to avoid it is over attentiveness by English officialdom to Irish ports. The instinct of the heart, however, is to first find out what you are up to, here.'

'I didn't know anybody was interested in me,' said Ritter. 'Honestly. But I promise you that the story I'm looking at isn't in any way related to the IRA, or to Irish politics, or even to British intelligence. I haven't the faintest idea why they should be looking for me, if in fact they are.'

'We don't want the British here at all, even on a temporary look out. What do you suggest we do about it?'

'If there's really a man from British intelligence at Dun Laoghaire, and if he's really waiting for me to go through the docks, he won't have long to wait. I'll be going through in a day or two. He can pick me up then. It isn't a problem for me.'

'There is of course another consideration. That is that if you are doing something which interests British Intelligence, as you surely seem to be, and if they are an annoyance, it would not worry us at all, especially if we had an inkling as to what was going on here, to arrange some way to – how should I put it? – to frustrate their knavish tricks.'

'Oh no,' said Ritter, 'I wouldn't want you to do anything like that, at all!'

After the men had gone, Ritter telephoned McKeown's home, and then contacted his news editor by dialling directly to one of the numbers of the newsroom phones near the news desk.

'How are things going?'

'Oh, bloody great. I don't know who's been talking to who now, but you've got double-o-bloody-seven scouring the Mountains of Mourne, looking for me.'

'How do you know that?'

'You wouldn't believe it, if I told you.'

'Kinnell! The bastards!'

'That's a great help, Bill.'

'Just keep your head down, Chas, I'll sort out what I can from this end. They haven't found you, though?'

'I'm sure that'll make all the difference! But, no, they haven't found me, yet.'

'You haven't got a location yet for what we're looking for?'

'I'll phone tomorrow.'

Ritter returned to the bar, ordered a pint of Guinness, and took it upstairs to his bedroom where he started to re-read his notes.

*

'I had a little walk round the cemetery this morning,' he told Doctor Morell when their conversation resumed the following day. 'It's neat, and it's small, and there haven't been a lot of deaths here, comparatively, since the end of the war.'

'I wouldn't really know about that.'

'You see, doctor, I've worked it out. There have been forty-two burials since the summer of forty-five.'

'If you say so.' The doctor looked genuinely puzzled.

Twenty-six of them, continued Ritter, were related to people already buried, so they went in family graves. Eleven were women or children. That left five. Five men, all over sixty, buried in the village cemetery. The reporter laughed. All he had to do now was check out those five men. Four of them would have been there since before the war, in fact during it. The other one would be the Führer.

'You see, you gave it away. You said "we'd earmarked this place earlier." See...? "We'd earmarked it..." Who earmarked it? You and the Führer, that's who. What's remarkable about this God-forsaken hole? Why would anybody earmark this place? – It's eleven hundred feet above sea level. What else is eleven hundred feet above sea level? Braunau am Inn is! Eleven hundred and fifty, actually, but near enough. Who believes that man works best at the altitude he was born – a cock-eyed theory if ever I heard one? – Your Adolf!'

'It is, I confess, an interesting conclusion, Mr Ritter.'

'I guess it is, at that, Doctor Morell. By the way, there's also a flaw in your clock-watching: how are you supposed to tell the time when somebody's hung a tea-towel over the clock?'

Dr Morell excused himself and said he needed to stretch his legs. He was going to the shop, he said, to buy some bread.

While he was out of the house Ritter turned to Mrs Morell. 'I don't suppose you'd like to save me some time, would you, and tell me which of the five graves it is I'm looking for?'

'I don't want to say anything,' she said. 'But I don't really think you want any of them.'

Ritter lunched in the pub on mutton stew and a couple of pints of Guinness, and managed to eliminate one of the five dead men in the cemetery simply by establishing that he had been the owner of the pub between 1930 and 1948. At four o'clock he made his daily check call to McKeown.

'I think I've found him. Well, sort of. More or less.'

'Terrific. But don't tell me over the phone.'

'No. I need a bit more time. Probably just until tomorrow.'

'Come back with it. Don't phone it. Do you want a monkey with you?'

'Not yet, there's nothing to photograph yet. And there's something I've just remembered. Speak to you later.'

Ritter hung up and walked out of the telephone kiosk and back to the Morell's house.

'Why,' he asked the doctor, 'didn't you buy any bread at the grocer's?'

'They were sold out.'

'They were not. They still have a loaf in the window.'

'Please understand, Mr Ritter, I am an old man. I went to the shop to buy bread and started to talk to the shopkeeper. I suppose I just forgot why I had gone in. Also, you should appreciate, all your constant questioning does not help me to concentrate on what I am supposed to be doing. I'll go over and buy one, now.'

'Too late,' said Ritter, looking across the street. 'The time by your ever-right Grocer's shop is twenty past four, and Mrs Brown has just taken the last loaf out of the window.'

SIX

Ireland is a state of mind. It is a slow-moving country and the only thing that is quick is the speed with which the slowness gets to you. Perhaps it was something to do with the time it takes to pour a pint of Guinness. Whatever, it certainly slowed Ritter down. He had four names in his notebook, now, to investigate. It was early June. The sun was hot and he felt there was no hurry.

He sat on the wooden bench by the bus stop: the village ran to a morning bus and an afternoon bus out, and a lunchtime bus and a teatime bus back. He mentally composed a postcard to his wife. *Haven't time to write a letter so am writing card; can't say much on a card so will close...* Too flip. To hell with it: *Here on a job. Roasting hot. Will ring when I get back. C.*

Pat Cooney, who helped behind the bar of the Badgers, joined him on the bench. He put a cardboard suitcase at his feet and propped a canvas-wrapped fishing rod against the back of the bench.

'Start my holidays today,' he told Ritter, patting the canvas bag. 'Get a few brownies.'

The reporter smiled. 'For a minute I thought you were going to get some young Girl Guides, 'til I saw the trout rod.'

He showed Pat the postcard, the picture was of a mother and foal, Irish Hunters. 'By the way, I've missed the collection this morning, Pat. Would you mind dropping this in a post box when you hit town?'

''Twill be a pleasure to do that for you,' said the barman, raising his fly-bedecked tweed hat, and he pocketed the postcard.

'Pat, did you know a chap who used to live around here, called Kelleher?'

'Kelleher, is it? Used to live round here, you say? Now, where would he be living these days?'

'Oh, he's dead, died twenty years ago.'

'Kelleher, you say? Now, what would you say his other name would be?'

Ritter checked his notebook. 'Thomas Peter.'

'And would he have been known, locally, and to his friends, as Thomas Kelleher, or Peter Kelleher?'

'I've absolutely no idea, Pat. But Thomas was his first name, so probably Tom, or Thomas.'

'Thomas Kelleher, you say... but probably Tom Kelleher.' He rubbed his chin in agonising thought.

At that moment the door of the Badgers opened and Maire, the landlady, stepped out into the sunshine.

'Maire, me darlin',' called Cooney. 'Do you recall old Tommy Kelleher at all?'

'Tommy Kelleher? Tommy Kelleher who came from Wicklow, and played the flute?'

'Now think, Maire. Would that have been Tommy Kelleher – or was that Peter Kelleher who played the flute?'

'I remember now. It was Tommy Calloway,' said Maire. 'The one who played the flute.'

Pat Cooney slapped his knee. 'That's the man, Charles! Tommy Calloway. I knew Maire would know him. What about him?'

'Not Calloway,' said Ritter, patiently. 'Kelleher.'

'There's nobody round here called Kelleher,' said Cooney. 'If I were you I'd stick to Calloway. That's a far better bet. And he plays the flute.'

'Why are you looking for Tommy Calloway?' asked the landlady. 'He doesn't live round here. He lives in Wicklow.'

Ritter wished Pat Cooney 'tight lines' during his fishing holiday, and went into the pub for a Guinness.

Maire, he had learned, was separated from her husband and the licence remained in his name. For this reason especially, according to pub gossip, Maire led a completely –

or apparently completely – chaste life; any hint at grounds for divorce could lead to her losing both pub and home. She managed the Badgers ably with the help of Cooney, a likeable though loquacious little man who each morning baked the bread for the village and sold it via Mrs Brown's shop. He had a perfect rapport with his boss, generally pre-empting her requests to change barrels or shift crates or collect glasses: Maire would look for Pat to give him the instruction and find him already doing it. But, if the barman sometimes tried to give the impression that their relationship was slightly more than that of master and servant, Maire appeared not to notice, or perhaps to ignore it. She was a popular, though tough, mine hostess, often pretending fierceness with her regulars. One day Ritter had been present when a motorist, clearly English and clearly lost, had asked her for directions and then for a whiskey. Maire had poured a generous measure and then, with a care for the heat of the day, offered ice.

'My dear, if the good lord had intended whiskey to be drunk with ice he would have arranged for it to be distilled in Iceland, not Ireland,' he replied, pompously.

Perfectly mimicking his accent, Maire had replied: 'And if the good lord had intended you to drink at my bar I would have served you, not barred you. Now be gone.' And with that she had pointedly poured the whiskey down the sink.

*

Father Dennis modestly drew his cassock across his khaki shorts to hide the white knees he had been exposing to the sunshine in his presbytery garden. When he realised that his afternoon visitor was Charles Ritter he pulled back the black hopsack and resumed his worship of the sun. Like most of the village by now, he had met Ritter at the bar of the Badgers and been alternately entertained and horrified by stories of Viet Nam and of Aberfan.

'I went over to see the Bishop, yesterday, my boy, and I told him your story about refusing the Yankee rifle. It surely tickled his grace. In spite of what they say across the water, decent stories in Ireland are rare enough, and the truth of the matter is that I made the journey to the Castle just to tell him about it.' Ritter's story, which had delighted the Badgers' audience on more than one occasion, revolved around his trip accompanying US Marines to a village in a Viet Nam demilitarised zone. Ritter had refused the offer of a US rifle and grenade belt on the grounds that, as a war correspondent, he should be non-combatant. The marine sergeant officially responsible for Ritter's safety, who looked and spoke like an eighteen-year-old Cassius Clay, finally yelled at him:

'Listen suh, if some VC bastard comes busting through here there's no way he's gonna pause and say "excuse me, bub, is you a news guy?"'

Father Dennis signalled to his housekeeper, who clearly understood that she should bring two glasses and a bottle of Frascati from the presbytery larder's cold shelf. And the two men sat chatting together in the sunshine, their long legs stretched out in the summer sun. The priest was the only man in the village taller than Ritter; at six feet six he was probably taller than anybody in Ireland. They talked about the weather; everybody was talking about the weather. They talked a little about different churches, and about different conceptions of God.

They talked at length about Father Dennis' hobby, casting bronzes for decorating homes and gardens. The priest had built a big kiln in the presbytery cellar, alongside the furnace that was used to heat both the house and the adjoining church. The church funded the high cost of fuel – the kiln, he explained, needed to reach a temperature of nearly one thousand degrees – but the church also benefited from the profits, so he reckoned it was a good deal. Then they talked about his other passion, horse racing, which, it appeared, usually produced less by way of profit.

'When you're on the phone to your head office, can you not ask the racing man for some tips? I don't get any help at all from *my* head office! It's a pity, though, that you weren't here on Saturday. I got a great tip during the wedding I was doing.'

'During it?' queried Ritter. 'You mean at the reception?'

'Not at all. The best man kept looking at his watch while I was conducting the service, so I asked him if he had a problem. He said he had a tip for the five o'clock race, and it was a certainty, but he hadn't had the chance to put a bet on.'

The priest raised the bottle to ensure he had Ritter's attention. 'Well, I tell you, Charles, it was a full nuptial, but I truly whistled through that service. At five to five the pair of us were over the hill and in the betting shop and at five past I was twenty-five pounds the richer. And if I'd been able to find the keys to the poor box – why, I might not be here talking to you now!'

Then they talked about the cemetery.

'Five old men died and were buried there since the war, actually since summer 1945,' Ritter told the priest. 'In fact, more than five died, but there were five who are buried alone, that is, not in family graves. One of them used to run the Badgers. Who are the others? Why should there be four old and single men dying here after the war?'

'Is it important?'

'It might be.'

'You'd better tell me their names.'

Ritter again referred to his notebook. The names were written for easy access on the inside of the blue card cover, rather than on the feint-ruled pages. He listed the names.

'Joe Breen, I buried myself,' the priest told him. 'His wife went to America to live with the daughter, and she's either still living there or perhaps, God rest the dear woman's soul, even buried there by now. The others died before I came to this parish. Kelleher and Cully, I've never heard of, not them nor their families.'

'And O'Toole?'

The priest laughed. 'You know, Charles, whatever you're doing in this parish, you're a welcome spirit; I'll tell you that. You, a reporter on a fine newspaper for well-educated Tories, and you sit there in that very spot and ask me how it can be that men here die old and single.'

He reached across and slapped Ritter across the shoulder. 'Michael Patrick O'Toole, who is buried in the corner of the cemetery beneath just a simple wooden cross, would be the priest that buried the other two. It was his parish before it was mine, and God willing I'll be another to die apparently single, and if the saints wish it, and the good lord spares me, also very old.'

*

The George, at Heddon on the Wall, Northumberland, stands in the fork at the start of the two optional routes from Newcastle upon Tyne to Carlisle, the A69 and the Military Road. It is not named after any of the half dozen king Georges, nor even after George Wade, the general who largely demolished Hadrian's Wall in order to build the 'military' road to transport ammunition from the Tyne's gun works – at Wallsend – to Carlisle where he urgently needed them to subdue the Scots. Rather, it was named after a local hero, George Stephenson, the engineer who also gave all Tynesiders the epithet, 'Geordie'.

It is an unprepossessing pub, intended for use as a local, rather than as a touristy 'country pub'. It was built out of the stone used for the Wall, and being set on solid rock had a 'cellar' above ground, and behind rather than below the bar. The 'snug' was also reached by lifting the hatch and passing behind the bar; it deterred strangers.

And strangers were easy to spot; more so if they assumed that everywhere north of the Trent was the Frozen North, and arrived wearing a Crombie coat in June. The dramatic effect was akin to a Western bar: as the stranger entered, the pub's pianist, midway through a tune called *Side Saddle*, stopped playing in order to get a better look at the visitor.

The stranger looked about him. Everyone in the bar was drinking beer. 'A pint of best, please.'

'Scotch?'

'No, sorry, I said a pint of best beer.'

'You'll want this, then,' said the landlord, and pulled him a pint of Newcastle Scotch Ale.

A little man, short and bow-legged, shoved his elbow into the stranger's Crombie-covered ribs, nodded at the foaming pint and told him: 'You'll not have tasted nothing like that doon sooth.'

'Passing through?' asked the landlord.

'I'll probably stay the night somewhere locally.'

'You can take your coat off, if you like, if you're stopping. Give it here, I'll hang it up for you.'

The stranger took off his coat to reveal a herringbone patterned double-breasted suit in grey. He held his pint glass up to the window, appreciatively.

'There's nothing wrong wi' that,' said the landlord, defensively.

'No. Quite. It's really very good.'

'There's no need to hold it up, then. There's nothing wrong wi' it at all.'

'You on business here?' The stranger turned around. This time it was the pianist addressing him.

'Sort of, yes. But I was in the Army with a chap who lived here. I thought I might look him up. Guy called Ritter, as a matter of fact.'

'You were in the Northumberlands, then,' said the short man; 'That's what young Charlie were in. You'll recognise some of the badges, here, then.' He indicated a promotional map of the north of England and its associated regiments – the Northumberland Fusiliers, the Durham Light Infantry, Green Howards, York and Lancasters, and others from the

Coldstreams to the Cheshires – who appeared to have in common the enjoyment of drinking Scottish and Newcastle Breweries' products.

'I were in the QDG's.' And when the stranger did not respond, the short man explained: 'The Queen's Dragoon Guards. I'm not Welsh, like, I wanted to be a groom, but they made me a mechanic, instead. I'll bet you were an officer, though.'

The stranger smiled, modestly.

'Let me get this filled up,' offered the pianist, adding 'What sort of business brings you here?'

'Nothing at all, really, just passing through. Thought I might look up an old pal.'

'He were in the Army with Charlie Ritter.'

'And Chas told you this is where he used to drink, did he?' The pianist appeared puzzled.

'Yes, that's the sort of thing.'

'When you knew him in the army?'

'That's right.'

'He doesn't live here now, you know,' it was the failed groom again. 'He did when he were demobbed, but he lives down London now. He just comes up to see his missus. She still lives here, at the bottom of the hill. She's a lovely lass, has horses, you know.'

'He's in our leek club, you know,' said the landlord. 'And he still pays his subs, though he doesn't live here, and he doesn't enter a stand any longer.'

'He never won anything, though,' said the mechanic. 'Last September my stand of onions came thirty-second.'

The pianist paid for the round and said: 'Nevertheless, it's surprising that he talked about this pub to his army friends.'

'Not really,' said the stranger. 'People get homesick doing national service.'

The pianist shrugged and carried his pint to the piano, sat down, and played a noisy version of the Animals' *House Of The Rising Sun*. He stayed seated at the piano stool and eventually, when the stranger left, he followed him to the car park behind the pub and watched him drive away.

*

Sue Ritter saddled her massive grey hunter, Bobbin, and drew him into the yard. She tightened his girth – geldings often expand their stomachs when a girth is fastened in the usually vain hope of avoiding any discomfort, so they need double-checking – cast her eye over the rest of the tack and climbed on to the stirrup and threw her long shapely leg over the saddle. It was a long way up: the horse had been bought by her husband for his own use when, in a last attempt to save the marriage, he had tried to share her passionate interest in riding. Bobbin had been bigger than her own mount, but he had cost more to buy, and when it came to a decision to sell one, it was her own she sold. At seventeen and a half hands the horse put his rider's seat six feet above ground level; and she was already tall. It would be a long way to fall, but she never fell off.

She wheeled the horse into the lengthy driveway, clicked her tongue to encourage him to move on, and trotted him along the winding gravel. To her annoyance there was a car blocking the gateway. People used it if making a U-turn on the narrow Carlisle road. She reined Bobbin in and waited. Then, realising that there was no exhaust issuing from the back of the car – a Ford Consul, and not one that she recognised as belonging to anyone in the village – she told the horse: 'Walk on,' and approached the driver impatiently.

She tapped the Consul's roof with her riding crop and, when the driver emerged, said: 'Would you mind moving this car, please? This is a private road.'

He doffed the blue trilby that matched his Crombie coat. 'You must be Mrs Ritter,' he said. 'I was in the Army with your husband.'

'I hope you haven't come specially to see him: he's in London.'

Sue Ritter did not see the necessity to explain the intricacies of her private life to strangers. 'If you want to see him, you'll have to contact him there.'

'It's not important, just that I was passing.'

'You can contact him at the *Post*.'

'Fine. Yes. I'll do that.'

'Now I'm afraid I'll have to ask you to move your car.'

The driver doffed his hat again, started the car and drove forward so that the horsewoman could move past him. She didn't feel it necessary to watch him drive away.

The consul was still blocking the drive when a small blue Morris van with Heddon Groceries stencilled on the side pulled in.

'Can you move the car, please?' asked a man in a khaki smock coat.

'Not at the moment. I'm afraid I've broken down.'

'But I've got to deliver these messages.'

The car driver looked at a box that had once held potato crisps.

'Messages?'

'Groceries,' the deliveryman translated.

'Well, if you like, I'll take them up the drive for you. I'm waiting for a mechanic.'

'You're a gent,' said the van man. 'They're not heavy. It's just the milk and the papers and a few groceries for the house at the end. And the mail – it saves the postman the trip, you know. Just put them in the porch if you don't mind. The lady of the house isn't in, I've just seen her going out on her horse.'

SEVEN

Ritter did not spot anyone conspicuously watching out for him at Dun Laoghaire, but he quickly noticed the dark green Rover 3.5, that moved in behind him as he drove away from the docks in Liverpool. It was a long drive to Fleet Street, consisting mostly of three-lane roads with the middle lane marked out for southeast and northwest drivers to overtake alternately. Ritter had the advantage on the bends, he could pull out quickly, just before overtaking became either illegal or difficult, or both, for the car behind; but the bigger car caught up on the straights. Before they were out of the midlands it had occurred to Ritter that there was no point in losing the car following him: the driver almost certainly knew that he was going to the office. He settled down at more or less thirty miles per hour in built-up areas, and at an average of ninety out of town.

He thought it might be fun to lose the Rover once he got into London, and managed to put two red buses and a taxi between them. But as he turned off Fleet Street and north up Fetter Lane, he spotted the dark green car ahead of him, parked opposite the plastic Sixties facade of the *Post*'s front door in Montague Court.

McKeown was waiting for him. They went first to Morris's office, and there they waited for the editor's secretary to ring and tell them that he was free to see them.

'I don't believe it. I honestly don't believe it.' Donald Porter, editor of the *Post*, clapped the heel of his hand against his en brosse shiny black hair. 'I mean to say, I mean, I am, after all, only the editor of this mighty newspaper. I'm only the person who has created the highest circulation for any serious newspaper in the entire western world. I am only the most successful editor in the history of Fleet Street. But you three,' he gestured towards Morris, McKeown, and Ritter, '...you three think "I know, we'll organise a bit of grave robbing, but we won't tell the old man until' we find MI-bloody-five chasing us all over Britain. No! – All over the United bloody Kingdom and Ireland including doorstepping the bloody office! – Because there's no bloody need for him to bloody know what we're up to...!" That's what you think! God, I need a drink!'

He opened a cupboard built in to his bookcases and reached for a bottle of Scotch. 'If you want any ice,' he told the other three, 'you'll have to go and get some.'

He poured himself a drink, and left the bottle and three glasses on a bookshelf for them to pour their own.

'Don't tell him you've got a world exclusive.' Morris had said before the three left his office for the editor's. 'He shits himself if you use that phrase. Just tell him it's a good story and let the idea develop in his own mind that it's only a really good story if we have it to ourselves.'

The meeting had started calmly. Jake had ushered McKeown and Ritter in to the sparsely decorated room with bound copies representing the ten years' issues that Donald Porter had edited. He had listened in wonder while Morris and McKeown and Ritter had told the story piecemeal. It was only at the end, when he realised that Ritter had the story to himself, that the *Post* had a scoop against the world, but with serious political implications, and in spite of the best efforts of the security services to discover what he was up to, that he became overawed by the enormity of the situation.

'You can't take on British Intelligence!' he stormed. 'I don't understand the game the three of you think you're playing. Who the hell do you think you are? There's only one way to play this, and that's to play it with the Security people. Not against them. Then, when they say it's a goer, and when they give you the all clear, you can run it. But you can't screw up MI5.'

'It's MI6, this one. And they'd screw us up, and Morell, if they had half a chance... if they had any idea where to find him,' Ritter told him.

'Charles,' said the editor, with a sigh, 'there is reporting, and there is editing. Reporting is reporting. It is collecting information, presenting it in a readable way, and somehow sending it to the paper. The decisions, the ones that are important, are editing decisions. Now... I don't tell you how to do your job because you are a very experienced and competent reporter who enjoys my total confidence, as a reporter, and does his job, as a reporter, admirably. And I trust that you will not presume to tell me, the most experienced editor in Fleet Street, an editor who might be thought by some to be not a complete arsehole and to have some idea what he is doing... I would appreciate it if you did not presume to tell me how to do my job. Is that understood?'

Ritter looked at McKeown and Morris in case either was going to speak. They were both staring fixedly at light fittings on the ceiling.

'It's not that,' said Ritter, eventually. 'One factor is that the story, while not compromising British security, will embarrass the intelligence services, MI6, anyway. They want to shut Dr Morell up. They might even lock him up. And they'd shut us out.'

'I'm warning you! Don't tell me my job!' said Porter. He poured himself another drink. 'What are we going to do?'

'Keep out of their way. I've got it down to two graves. Morell will tell me if I keep at him. Meanwhile we should get pictures of the cemetery, the graves and the headstones.'

'Don't tell me what to do! If you do that again, you can get out of the office!'

'It's right that we have to keep out of their sights,' said McKeown. 'We're so near that it would be wrong to lose control now.'

'Don't tell me what's right and wrong! I know what's right and wrong, for God's sake!' He gulped his drink.

'The best thing,' said Morris, 'is if we play this on our own for the time being, get it sorted, and sorted properly, and when we've got it right, we liaise with security, and then we organise with them how we're going to put it out.'

'Thank you, Jake,' said Porter. 'That's exactly what I was going to suggest. In fact, I think it's what I said earlier. Thank God for one sane voice in the office! You've all heard what we're going to do, now get on with it. It was Jake's decision, remember, and not mine. I'm handing this one over for Jake to run, since he's the one whose thinking appears to be straightest, and in line with mine.'

'The editor's indecision is final,' said McKeown when they were back in Morris' office.

'I suppose all he really cares about is his knighthood,' muttered Ritter into his glass.

'And his job, for God's sake. If he sees this year out he'll retire, and then he'll be the first *Post* editor to retire voluntarily.'

'I thought he was sacked once.'

'He was,' Morris confirmed. 'And he got a pay-off. He went to El Vino to drown his sorrows and when he came out of the door he found the Old Man waiting for him in the limo with a cheque for his pay-off, and a letter offering him his job back on more pay.'

At that moment the door opened and Porter came in.

'I've been thinking,' he said... 'You say we let Hitler escape. But who was responsible?'

'Military intelligence,' said Ritter.

'I mean, was Labour in power by then, or was it us?' – The *Post*, which publicly claimed to be an independent newspaper, privately considered itself an intimate part of the Conservative Party.

'It didn't just happen on one specific day,' said Ritter. 'It went on over several months. What month was the 1945 election?'

'July. Election day was the fifth.'

'A bit of each, then. But either way, Military Intelligence wouldn't have been checking back with Whitehall.'

'In any case, it's not a political thing. It's only Int who will be bothered,' said McKeown.

'You think so, do you? Don't you think world reaction will encompass more than the cloak and dagger merchants when we announce that Britain let Hitler go? Don't you think they'll ask for the head of every general, every war minister, every prime minister and every spy boss since 1939 – and be right to?'

'The Americans are as much, if not more, to blame, I'd say,' offered Ritter.

'When you write it, for God's sake make sure you make it clear, in that case, that it was the Americans who were to blame. Lay it on with a trowel. And remember,' he said to Morris as he reopened the door, 'I'm handing this one entirely over to you, as my deputy.'

When the editor had closed the door McKeown asked: 'Kinnell, Jake! He hasn't got a deputy. Has he just appointed you deputy editor, do you reckon?'

'Not a hope. He's just appointed me Executive Editor (Blame).'

Morris searched around in a cupboard, which contained a tape recorder, a camera, a pair of shoes and several dozen back numbers of the *Post*, and finally produced a bottle of red wine.

'Plonk,' he said, withdrawing the cork with an attachment on his penknife.

'The first time I had plonk,' said Ritter, 'I was told it was called that because after two glasses you go plonk.'

'It's only the office Beaujolais,' said Morris. 'So you might well go plonk. Drink it before it gets cold.'

'We've got to get a team together,' said McKeown. He had removed his spectacles from his face, in readiness for chewing. 'Minders, snappers, all that. What do you think you need, Ritter?'

'A couple of heavies for when the story breaks,' suggested Ritter. 'It's a pity Fergy's not here.'

'Well, you can't have Ferguson,' he's still sitting in Tel Aviv waiting for the bloody war to start. Don't forget you've got Dublin office. Plus Belfast, if you need 'em. By the way,' continued McKeown, 'I don't know how this thing has got out in Germany, but there's a guy chasing you from *Die Welt*. Seems he knows all about the doctor. The security on this everywhere is rubbish. Anyway he's here in town, this kraut, and wanting you to call him. I said you were out of town and I didn't know when to expect to hear from you. How does this guy know anything?'

'That's OK; that's Bayer. He's the one I told you about, the one who did the original research when we didn't know there was anything at all. I'll fill him in on the day we run the story, I owe him that, but that's all.'

'But he's here. In Fleet Strasse.'

'No problem. He won't find me.'

Ritter went home to the basement flat in Marloes Road to collect his mail and a change of clothes. As he turned the Chubb key he found it already unlocked. He pushed the door; it was locked on the Yale; he and Ferguson always double locked the door when they went out.

Gingerly, he slid the Yale key in and opened the door. There was someone moving about inside.

'Who's in there?' he shouted. 'Come on, who is it?'

'Oh, hello, Mr Ritter. It's only me.' It was Mrs Yarranton, who cleaned the flat for the two journalists.

'There's a lot of mail for you, on the table. And there've been two callers for you: a young foreigner, German, I'd say, only he's very smartly dressed, and a man wanting to sell burglar alarms and the like.'

'Bayer? Did the German say if his name was Bayer?'

'He didn't say. He said he'd come back. So did the burglar alarm man, and he's already been back. I told him he should go and see the landlord.'

'Quite right, love,' Ritter told her. Although he knew the chance of his landlord forking out from the rent for a burglar alarm would be verging on the remote.

'And there's a note from Mr Ferguson, on the mantlepiece.'

Ritter read it. It was a note he had left for his flatmate itemising household bills he had paid during the previous month. Ferguson had drawn a ring around the line which said the window cleaner had been paid three shillings, and commented: *Why should I pay? I never get to look out of them!*

Ritter smiled and put the paper in a drawer as the doorbell rang.

Two men in sports jackets and flannels stood like Laurel and Hardy at the foot of the steps which led from pavement level to the door of the basement flat.

'Mr Ritter?' asked the chubby one, with hair placed carefully across his balding scalp, like Bobby Charlton.

'Who wants him?'

'We're from Double-S Security. We wondered whether you might be interested in making your flat more secure, bearing in mind the number of break-ins there's been in the area, recently.'

'No thanks.' Ritter moved to shut the door.

'We'd like to come in and talk to you about it,' said the tall thin one.

'No thanks.'

'Seriously, Mr Ritter – you are Mr Ritter, aren't you? – Security is a big problem round here for people like you who work away from home a lot.'

'Who works away from home a lot?'

'You do.'

'Who says I do?'

'Now, now, sir. We do our research.' He put his hand around the edge of the door.

'If you did any research, at least, if you did it thoroughly, you'd know there was nothing in here worth pinching.'

'If we can just come inside and talk...'

From the pavement came a familiar accented voice: 'How's tricks, you old bastard? Hang on, I'm coming down!'

Ritter looked up to see the welcome face of Hermann Bayer. 'Come on in, old mate. I'll open a bottle of something!'

He turned to the two men. 'Sorry, I've got a visitor. As you can see.'

'That's all right,' said the security man. 'We'll come back later.'

Ritter took two pint bottles of Newcastle Amber Ale – the lighter version of Newcastle Brown – opened both, and filled half-pint glasses for his visitor and himself. Pint bottles and half-pint glasses was the Geordie way.

Mrs Yarranton, who declined the offer of a drink, said: 'That's the men who were here earlier. A bit persistent, if you ask me. They must be on commission.'

'They were here when I came round, this morning,' said Bayer. 'They've been waiting for you to come in.'

'How long have you been here, Hermann? Didn't know you knew my home address.'

'I didn't, but I knew your number, so I looked it up in the reverse directory at the office to find your address. I came round about opening time, and just sat in the beer garden across the road, enjoying your English weather. Those two were sitting in their car – it's a Cortina – sweltering. If you ask me, they're either private dicks or even your national front lot, or both.'

'Why do you think that?'

'Because that's what they'd be if we were in Germany. They all look alike, you know.'

Ritter refilled the glasses. 'Well, thanks for turning up when you did. What are you doing in London, anyway? I've got nothing to tell you.'

'Well, I've got some information for you.' Bayer took some sheets of folded foolscap from his jacket pocket and handed them to Ritter. 'It's some additional background on your Doctor Morell. Everything's there except one fact.'

'Which is?'

'Where he is now.'

Ritter laughed. 'When I asked you that, you said he'd be in Hell, most likely.'

'But you and I now know differently, Charles; we know that he's in Ireland.'

'That's a good story, Hermann. If I were you, I'd write it.'

'Oh I will, my dear Charles. I will. As soon as I find him. Or sooner, if you share the information with me, as you promised.'

'Why do you think he's in Ireland, Hermann?'

'If you confirm I'm right, I'll tell you.'

'Nope, sorry. We both know that Morell died on his way out of the bunker. We've seen the paperwork. My interest in him was totally coincidental to anything else. The plain truth is, I suffer, or suffered, from this killer-migraine, and I thought Morell might have had something in his dossier that would cure it.' That was the plain truth, or at least, certainly not a lie.

'Bollocks. OK, Charles. Have it your way. Keep the dossier I gave you, as a little gift. It might come in handy – just, as you say, coincidentally.'

'Anyway, Hermann, thanks for looking in, especially when you did.' Ritter picked up his bag and headed for the door with Bayer. He turned to Mrs Yarranton: 'Your money's on the mantlepiece. Sorry, there's a couple of extra glasses to wash now, on the draining board. I don't know when I'll be back...'

He followed Bayer up the stone steps onto Marloes Road and threw his bag of clean laundry on top of the newspapers on the back seat.

'Keep in touch, Hermann. I'll tell you when I have something. I'll ring you at the office. In Hamburg!'

He closed the door of the Rapier gently, and set off up the street past St Mary Abbots Hospital. Behind him, a Cortina pulled out and the driver honked his horn angrily as he found his way blocked by a red Audi with German plates laboriously executing a three-point turn.

By the time the road was clear the Sunbeam was lost in the traffic of Kensington High Street.

*

Ritter had rung his wife and told her he was heading north. As expected, she had invited him to stay at the house they once shared. But, first, he had to talk to his mother.

He stopped at Bookless's to buy a bouquet of a dozen short-stemmed roses in assorted colours, and then drove down Westgate Road with them on the seat beside him. It had been a long time since they'd chatted. He thought that she might recognise his footfall, as he approached.

'It's me, *Mutti*... I have been back in Berlin – at least, I've been there mentally. Before the war, and at the end of it. It's weird, you know. It's a great story. I mean, you're not gonna believe this, but Hitler didn't die in Berlin after all! He didn't! Honestly! That's my story – what we call a scoop. He was spirited out at the end of the war and – you are not gonna believe this, either – it was the Brits that did it, and the Vatican too! And he ended up in Ireland... and I'm the only person who knows this, so I'm just trying to work out how and where he was actually buried, and that will be a world scoop! I'll be famous! You'll be proud. It means that all those stories – the suicide with Eva and killing the dogs, and maybe even the wedding, were probably all untrue. And that the body the Russians think they have, and did the autopsy on, was all phoney. You know, when the Russians announced that Hitler was...'

He had to be careful, here, talking to a lady. But his mother would probably not know the medical expression, monorchid... He thought for a moment, and then decided that, in the circumstances, she wouldn't be offended.

'...That Hitler had only got one ball... er... testicle... And we sang a song about it at school. Well, you probably didn't know that we sang it! Anyway I'm interviewing this German guy. He cured my migraine – would you believe that? One injection and the headaches stopped. I think they've stopped for good. You won't believe it, but he was Hitler's doctor – he really was! – his personal physician. Before that, he was a fairly famous doctor on the Ku-damm. He had a brass plaque with his name on it. You might even have seen it.'

You might even have met him, Ritter thought. Before her marriage his mother had been a senior secretary in the British embassy. A stunning blonde, as he knew from the disappointingly small collection of photographs she had preserved from those days, she had been invited to lots of parties in central Berlin. She had met film stars and opera singers and diplomats; it was highly likely that Morell would have been at some of them, invited by his patients.

'He's told me all about life in the early part of the war. The anti-aircraft guns on all the roofs, not needed for years. How they still showed Clark Gable films at the Marmorhaus; how they introduced rationing – although, he says, there was usually plenty of stuff around – bread, cocoa, eggs, flour, all that – and rationing was just to prevent hoarding, he said, but there were cards for soap and coal and shoes. He told me sometimes the shopkeepers used to open tins on the counter when they sold them – just so that people couldn't hoard them. It made me wonder whether you ever saw that. He used to grow his own vegetables in a little garden, *Mutti*. Like we did. Only nobody stole theirs. And his wife used to bake almond cakes. Like you did. And he remembers how the summers were always good and people used to go off most days to the parks and the lakes... and skating and sledging in Tiergarten in winter, just like we did.'

His mother, Ritter believed, must have had at least a few good memories of those days. Even if only one or two. He wanted to bring some back, and share them with her now. He had spent far too few precious days in her company.

She had had a lousy war. Widowed within the first few months, with a young son to bring up, an outcast in an enemy country. War could mean only excitement for a little boy, but stark terror for an enemy alien on her own. And Ritter was the man of the house; he would look after things, he had thought, on being told that his father was not coming back. But in this, Ritter had failed completely. He had tried to pull the bed-covers over his head to hide the sound of his mother's screams when she was beaten and raped in the next bedroom by German soldiers – as punishment for the heinous crime of being English. Less than a year later, curled up and sobbing in a corner of their kitchen, he had watched, totally helpless, as this time Russian soldiers had raped and sodomised his mother on the kitchen table for the crime of being apparently German. This time, his mother had not uttered a sound: possibly because her little son was in the same room; more likely, because she had no tears left to cry.

After all that, could there really be any 'Good Old Days' that she would have retained in her memory bank? Had she been, as the Morells had been, to see *Vom Winde Verweht*, 'from the wind blown about', which was how the Germans translated *Gone With The Wind*? The sunshine and the flowers, sailing model boats on the river... and later the cuddling together in their cellar while the RAF bombers whined overhead, and the Russian guns thundered into the city. It had been frightening – although not too much to a small boy who understood so little about danger – but they had always been together: that had been the best bit.

'It will soon be over *Karli*, it will soon be over... then I will take you home, to England!'

Ritter placed the small bouquet in an earthenware jar. He said 'Love you lots; love you always, *Mutti.*' Then he stood, wiped his eyes and walked down the drive and back to his car. Minutes later he passed the playground of his old junior school, and started whistling the march known as *Colonel Bogey*. Then he burst into song. He couldn't help it.

'Hitler had only got one ball.
Goering had two, but very small.
Himmler, had something sim'lar,
But poor old Goebbels... had no balls at all.'

*

Sue Ritter looked at her husband. 'Been to the grave?' He nodded.
'How was it?'
'Everything's fine.'
'Better go and dab your eyes with a cold flannel. They're all red and puffy.'
When he returned he asked, 'How are you... How's Dobbin?' He knew that how one was, depended very much on the other.
'Bobbin.'
'Dobbin. He was my horse; I bought him; I named him.' Their deal had been that he would get the car and she would get the horse.
'Now he's my horse: it's your car and it's my horse, and he's called Bobbin. You can call your car anything you like.'
'I think McKeown will give me a company car, if I want one.'
'I bet he won't give you a firm's Rapier.'
'I think it's Anglias and Vivas, but he might give me a Triumph Herald because there's a bit more leg room.'

'You! In a Herald! Don't be stupid. Just save up all your expenses instead of wasting them on drink, and you can buy a newer Sunbeam.'

'That's what Fergy's dad told him. He said: "Look at you – you don't smoke, you hardly drink, you don't back horses, you don't go out with wild lasses... I don't know, you just waste your money!" ...Of course, he didn't know much about his own son. Do you want to eat out?'

'Not particularly. There's plenty to eat here. I've a couple of fillets in the fridge. But we can go down to the George first, if you like.'

'OK. I wouldn't mind a decent pint.'

As they walked up the drive Sue told him about the visitor she had found parked in it. It was nobody Ritter could readily identify from her description. And at the bar of the George the would-be groom also told him about the man in the Crombie coat.

'Just a minute' – it was the man from the grocer's shop – 'Did he have a red Consul?'

'He did,' said the man who usually played the piano. 'With a Southampton registration number.'

'Didn't you have to go out and fix it?' asked the grocer. 'He was broken down and waiting for a mechanic.'

'He wasn't broken down when I saw him,' said Sue Ritter.

'Well he carried your groceries up the hill for me because I couldn't get past. There was nothing missing, was there?'

'Groceries, milk, cigarettes, papers, and a postcard from Ritter, that's all,' she said. 'I wasn't expecting anything else. Thanks for the postcard, by the way. What were you doing in Ireland? – There was nothing in the paper since the bombed farms.'

'IRA,' said the mechanic. 'I expect he was writing about the IRA again.'

'You wouldn't believe me if I told you,' Ritter told his wife.

'Better not tell me, then.'

'Oh: cigarettes,' said Ritter, as the publican routinely placed a packet of twenty on the bar. 'That reminds me, I've stopped smoking.'

'Christ!' said Sue Ritter, the landlord, the pianist, and the mechanic, as with one voice.

*

Cutting through a fillet steak in the dining room of their marital home, Ritter asked his wife: 'Seeing anybody?'

Instead of replying, she asked, 'How's Monica?'

'Oh, fine. I'll tell her you were asking kindly after her. You?'

'Yes. But I'll see to you tonight, if you like.'

Following her to the staircase, Ritter suddenly turned back. 'You've forgotten these.'

He picked up a packet of Rothmans.

'Leave them. If you can stop smoking, I'm damned sure I can.'

Ritter flicked over the postcard on the mantlepiece, read the postmark, and smiled at the thought that Cooney had gone all the way to his fishing village, before remembering to post it.

Later, in bed, Sue asked him. 'So, what do you do after that, if you can't have a cigarette?'

'Interestingly, I find that since I stopped smoking, I can just start all over again.'

Sue ran a hand down his body. Rubbing a square-cut fingernail along his inner thighs quickly stirred him back into action.

'I tend to forget that you're rigged like a horse.'

'Good job only the one of us is gelded.'

'If I am not having a cigarette,' she said, 'I'm going to need something else.' And she wriggled down the bed.

*

The one hundred and fifty miles to Stranraer was what the Sunbeam Rapier was designed for: tight and narrow, bend after bend, from Gretna to the docks. It was not what the Austin Cambridge, with its comfortable soft suspension, which pulled in behind Ritter at the end of his drive, was designed for: the car rocked and rolled with the bends and dips in the A69 and the A75. Every time he looked through his rear view mirror Ritter could see the man behind him gulping like a rider on a roller coaster.

He was in plenty of time for the Larne ferry, but he hung back and let the Austin get ahead of him in the queue, then allowed two other cars to get between them, for boarding. Precisely as he had been told to do.

He sat on the deck in the sunshine thinking about Sue. It had been good to see her; it was always good to see her. Sex with her familiar body was the best: it was always the best. The incredibly strong thighs she had developed in a lifetime spent mainly on horseback could control a massive Hunter, and control a husband, too. Ritter knew – she had told him – that she could bring herself to orgasm on the bridge of her Snowballs leather saddle, simply by holding on with her thighs and ordering the gelding to 'trot on'. She was an eager and vocally-appreciative sexual partner; thank goodness for a detached house with thick stone walls. Perhaps... if... but she wouldn't give up her riding, it was selfish to expect that, and he didn't want to live outside London, where all the best jobs were. Not yet, anyway.

Ritter pulled Bayer's papers out of his pocket and started to read.

Morell, the file said, was considered by all his colleagues to be a quack. They actually blamed him for Hitler's declining health during the war.

For Hitler's stomach cramps, he had prescribed Mutaflor, made by Hageda of Berlin, an emulsion of a strain of Escherichia coli, which neutralised the pains by aiding digestion. It was a controversial treatment at the time, and remained so today.

He prescribed Prostakrinium, a hormone product, extract of seminal vesicles and prostata, to prevent depression and fatigue, and another, Orchikrin, which combined various male hormones, plus extracts of testis, seminal vesicles and the prostata of young bulls. Both products were manufactured by Hamma of Holmutz.

There was Sympatol, from Boehringer, used to quicken the heart; Vitamultin, Morell's own product, containing pervitin and caffeine, to combat fatigue; Ultraseptyl, a sulphonamide drug made by Morell's firm in Budapest, was prescribed against colds and infections, but said to be harmful to the nerves.

What interested him were two products made by Merck, Darmstadt, the firm he had seen on Morell's bottle. Eukodal, a synthetic morphine derivate, was prescribed instead of morphine for severe pain, and Eupaverin, a synthetic alkaloid anti-convulsant made from poppies, used for spasms and peripheral blood disorders.

Morell mixed them to make a cocktail for intravenous injection.

Either, or both – or neither – could have been the drug Morell had given Ritter.

But reading on he came to Optalidon, from Sandoz of Nuremberg, a painkiller and analgesic Morell prescribed for Hitler's headaches.

So Ritter was no wiser. It occurred to him that, since Morell had said it was unlikely that he would need further treatment, the prescription didn't matter. Nevertheless, it would have been nice to have made a positive contribution to medical science by passing the information on to the Migraine Centre people in Charterhouse Square.

And then there were Dr Koester's Anti-Gas Pills, to prevent gas build-up, about which Ritter already knew. According to Bayer's papers, these contained strychnine and belladonna, and were believed by Morell's colleagues, Giesing and Brandt, to have been slowly poisoning the Führer. The pills, they said, could certainly have caused the intestinal disorders they were designed to relieve, and also the gradual discolouration of Hitler's skin. The two doctors concluded that Morell was slowly poisoning their leader. But the Führer's reaction, when they reported this to him, had been to banish them from his circle.

There were several pages pursuing this theme, and then Bayer's revelation that Morell had not died in Berlin, as reported by Axmann, but had escaped Germany, at least as far as Rome.

How the German journalist had established this, without having met Morell, intrigued Ritter. And how did he know about Ireland?

The medical information might intrigue his colleague McDairmid. But would it rock them in Rotherham? That's what Jake Morris always asked, when testing a story. Jake had never been to Rotherham, and in fact it was not a particularly good circulation area for the right-of-centre *Post*. But everybody knew what he meant. Would the readers go for the story? Well, everybody liked medical stories, these days, but the names of the treatments, as Morell himself had said, were not really important. Perhaps, Ritter thought, he could do a bit of freelancing, for once, and sell the medical details to the *New Scientist*, or the *British Medical Journal*. Who knows? – It might pay for a holiday, if he ever took one.

When the ferry sidled in to Larne and passengers were asked to go to their cars, Ritter donned his blazer and waited until the man with the Austin took his place at the wheel, before descending the staircase. The Austin's mirror picked up the tall, spare man in blazer and flannels who climbed into the Rapier, and moments later the cars were beckoned forward to the ramp and driven ashore one by one.

The Austin, first off, drove through the dock gates and pulled towards the kerb, allowing three cars to pass. He pulled in behind the third, the two-tone blue Rapier, and sat on its tail.

Travelling at speed, the two cars were well away from Larne by the time that Ritter, driving a grey Morris 1100 which had been the last car to board, and was – it amused Ritter to think – effectively an IRA staff car, disembarked.

Ritter drove to Belfast, and then to another Newcastle, the one in County Down, where he was staying the night with McKeown's brother.

The Rapier and Austin Cambridge also went to Belfast, and turned off towards Lisburn and then south to Craigavon. Just outside the town the Rapier suddenly accelerated ahead and a tractor and trailer pulled between the two cars. It was doing a steady ten miles an hour.

When the Austin driver sounded his horn in an effort to attract the tractor driver's attention, the farmhand yanked at a length of red baling twine and somehow slipped the tow bar, leaving the trailer askew in the middle of the narrow road, and drove on.

An hour later, the Austin driver telephoned to London. 'We've lost him, Ted, somewhere outside Craigavon, travelling south.'

'Bloody amateurs! Lucky for you, we know where he's going.'

*

Sunday, June 4, 1967. London.

McKeown was on the phone to his brother's home, talking to Ritter.

'We need to know the name of the village, now, so we can brief the phots and the minders.'

'I don't need them yet.'

'Well, it's about time you told us. Kinnell, Tex... It's not just a matter of what you need. Let's get things in perspective, here. There's an editor, a managing editor, and your friendly news editor – me. And there's a reporter – you. It's you that works for us, remember? Not the other way about. In any case,' he thought he'd try a diplomatic tack, 'what if you were run over by a bus?'

But Ritter explained that there were only a couple of buses where he was operating, so that prospect was unlikely. 'And what you need to remember, Bill,' he added, 'is that your building – yours and Jake's and the editor's building – leaks like a fucking sieve.'

McKeown was still listening to a dead telephone when the news desk told him he had a caller waiting, and it was somebody who had known him in Berlin. He had to rack his brain, even after failing to recognise the voice and getting the caller to identify himself as Rudi Mueller, to remember him as a small-scale black-marketeer in the Tiergarten quarter. Mueller was persistent about a meeting at pub opening time – seven o'clock on Sundays – and McKeown conceded he would join him in the Glue Pot, 'for just the one'.

They chatted about the Middle East crisis and Mueller assured him, claiming unattributed inside knowledge, that there would be no war. Then McKeown's stomach churned when Mueller said: 'And now I'm told you have a great scoop on your hands, Bill, my old chum. A Hitler scoop, no less!'

'What's this, Rudi?'

'Dr Morell, of course.'

'I don't know about that, Rudi.'

'You've got your man, the German speaker, er, Ritter, working on it, I know all about it. I have some friends, you know, who would be interested in buying some details early from you. German friends, back home.'

'It doesn't cost much to buy a copy of the *Post*, Rudi.'

'But when Ritter comes back – or will he file direct...?'

'He won't file from bloody Ireland, that's for sure!' It was Mueller's use of the word 'file', McKeown decided later, that had thrown him. It was an 'in' word, an office expression, used generally only by intimates. He said quickly: 'He won't file from bloody Ireland, he won't file from Scotland, nor from Wales, nor England. He'll bring his copy, whatever it is, into the office.'

It was bluster, and blatant bluster. And McKeown knew it hadn't fooled Mueller for one moment. Ritter was right: the building leaked like a fucking sieve. And he had just been responsible for some almighty fucking leaking. He was suddenly grateful that he didn't know the details of Ritter's whereabouts: that way he couldn't divulge them. He hurriedly excused himself on the grounds of pressure of work. Back at the news desk, he telephoned Berlin Military Headquarters.

'Colonel Wakefield, please... What?... Then put me through to his home...'

While the connection was being made he jotted down a few names.

He had told Ted.

Jake had told somebody, presumably somebody in the Israeli embassy in Kensington Palace Green.

Ritter himself had told Bayer.

Ted had told his office: he had no choice in the matter.

The Israeli embassy would have passed the information on to whomever.

Bayer would have – must have – told somebody in his office, otherwise he wouldn't be here in London.

Somebody, somewhere, somehow, had told Rudi Mueller.

Who else knew? How much had Ritter said to the medical editor? Had anybody in the library put two-and-two together about the cuttings Ritter – and then McKeown himself – had asked for? Would the editor tell anybody? Had he already warned the chairman? Had any of these people mentioned the extraordinary story to their wives? And who might the wives have told?

Kinnell! Ritter was right. The building leaked like a fucking sieve. Now the important thing had to be to rebuild some fences, to protect the story and, come to that, to protect Ritter who, McKeown realised, didn't know the half about the leakage.

The phone clicked. '...Tim? It's Bill McKeown... Yes, fine... I saw Rudi Mueller in London today. What's he up to these days? Still black marketeering, is he?'

Tim Wakefield told McKeown he didn't see people like Mueller so much as he used to. '...Not since they built the Wall.'

McKeown decided that if Ritter – quite rightly, he now believed – would not tell him where he was, he needed to know pretty quickly where he was not.

EIGHT

Sunday, June 4, 1967. Ramat Gan.

Meir Amit called the leading members of the Eichmann squad in to Mossad headquarters in Ramat Gan along the Netanya road, leading north out of Tel Aviv, and told them he had a special mission in mind.

The team was led by a former commando called Uri who had first seen action at the age of twelve. Others were members of the original *Hanokmin*, or were the relatives of people who had died in concentration camps; that was why they had volunteered to go after Eichmann.

'We're not looking for a man this time: we are looking for a grave. I'm afraid we have to desecrate the grave. We need the body, or the bones, brought here and we will have to arrange a certificated destruction of whatever the remains consist of. Then they will be scattered, probably over an ocean, so that not even one atom of the original exists.'

'Whose can this grave be?' asked the ex-commando.

'Adolf Hitler's.'

'That's crazy.'

'Perhaps it is better if we continue to think that it is crazy,' Amit told him. 'The first problem is that we don't know where the grave is. The second is that we don't know how to extract the remains when we find it. The third is that we are not the only people looking. How are we going to set this up? How many people do we need for the team?'

'Eli can organise finding the grave. He'll find it if anybody can. I'll do the grave robbing. If it's a case of rushing something back, or doing it secretly at any rate, we'll need back-up from the airforce, perhaps, to get the remains back here.'

'You can't have the airforce. They're going to be busy.'

Uri raised an eyebrow; was he about to miss some action? – 'El Al, then.'

'No.'

'Diplomatic bag?'

'Perhaps. From Germany, maybe. Austria, possibly. Mainland Europe certainly. That's my best guess.'

'Give Eli four telephones and four researchers as back-up, if he wants them. And four heavies standing by for me. Are you sure this is serious?'

'Deadly.'

'I'll get Eli started right away.'

*

Bobby Sanchez had skimmed so many hedgerows that he'd taken a coat of paint off the grey Triumph 2000 by the time he'd reached Stranraer. By the time he'd motored south from Larne and passed a totally unexpected – by him – Customs post on the road between Belfast and Dublin, he had lost his natural bonhomie.

'First of all,' he told the Company's Dublin staffer, when he had finally reached the office, 'they send me to Dunkirk to watch a fool from Six who's looking out for a blue car. I'm telling you! A blue car's about all he knows from nothing! Then it turns out he's looking for something called a Rapier, which is a coupe that looks like a sawn-off Jaguar. And what's he supposed to do when he sees this Rapier? He's supposed to follow it to an office in Fleet Street, London, and he already knows the address! Then he's supposed to follow it back to Dunkirk and see where it goes from there! And I'm supposed to follow both idiots!'

'Why didn't you just stake out the Fleet Street address and wait for a blue Rapier?'

'Are you asking me that? Do you want to know why? Because I only just found out what the Six game-plan was,

that's why. My job was to watch Six and see what happened.
And then what happens?'

'What happens?' His partner realised that the only way
was to humour him.

'What happens is that the aforementioned Rapier hasn't
been, and furthermore is not going, anywhere near little old
Dunkirk. Why not? Because Six doesn't know the difference
between Dunkirk, where the Rapier isn't, and Dublin, where
it plainly is. So, dear old Six tails said Rapier across the sea
to Ireland – and loses it. And we call these idiots Friends!'
He shook his head in despair. 'Did you know I was at West
Point?'

'I'd heard.'

'General George Armstrong Custer was at West Point,
and was thirty fourth out of a class of thirty four. Did you
know that? No. General Dwight D Eisenhower came sixty-
first out of a hundred and sixty four. Ulysees S Grant was
twenty-first out of thirty-nine. Do you know what I was?'

'Let me guess…'

'I was first. Out of ninety-three. Exactly the same as
General Douglas MacArthur. And just look at me now!'

'You should have stayed in the army.'

'I would've. Believe me, Ben; I would've.' Sanchez
pointed to his left eye. 'If I hadn't lost this, I'd've been a bird
colonel by now. A one-star general, maybe. Not fannying
about chasing Brits.'

'Look, Bobby, do you want to tell me the military history
of the US or only the full volume history of the Special
Relationship in this office, or do you want to get in the car
and find the man we're looking for, the actual Mr Charles
Ritter?'

'Jesus! Don't tell me you've found him.'

'More or less. At least I know where he is.'

'And those limey clowns are still searching the bogs of
Ireland for him?'

'I'll tell you about it on the way. You're in luck. It's a lovely little village he's staying in.'

Sanchez and his colleague put their suitcases in the boot of the Triumph and drove southwest out of Dublin.

'Yikes, don't hold out on me! Tell me how you found him.'

'It was inspiration, that's all. The guy we're looking for is a newspaperman, right? And newspapermen travel in packs, like jackals.' It was the Dublin man's turn to spin out a story. So, this man Ritter is on an assignment in Ireland for his paper, the London *Post*. And the London *Post*, like all the other London papers, has a bureau in Dublin. So, what does he use for back-up?'

'The Dublin bureau?'

'Precisely. So I went to the Dublin bureau.'

'And asked where in hell Ritter is? And they told you?'

'They aren't in the office, are they?' He paused to light a cigarette while negotiating the light traffic of the Irish capital. '...So where do you find newspapermen when they're not in the office?'

'In bed with some floozy?'

'In a bar, that's where. Same as New York, same as DC, same as journos anywhere in the world, I guess.'

He was enjoying extending the tale, but, thought Sanchez, there's God-all else to do while he's driving.

'So you found them in a bar.'

'Nope. I went to the bar they all use in Dublin and – by the way, the *Post*'s men in Dublin are called Kerrigan and Connolly – and I asked if anybody had seen them. And what did I discover?'

'That they were lying sloshed under a couple of bar stools?'

'That they had been sent out of town on what they call a baby-sitting operation. Which is exactly what you and I would call a baby-sitting operation. In other words, they've got somebody under wraps and they've got to protect their property.'

'You mean they've got a hot property and they've told people in the bar when they've got it? Are they as dumb as their security people?'

'Wrong, Bobby. Didn't West Point teach you anything about European history? SIS – or MI6 as the blatts here call it – is not Ireland's security service. Sometimes, in fact it's just the opposite. Anyway, these guys in the Dublin office, they only told one other newspaperman. He's a freelancer called Foley. He's the guy they've left looking after their patch for them. He's the only guy they thought needed to know.'

'So where are we going now?'

'To the most beautiful part of all Ireland, some say the most beautiful part of the world. It's a little village called Kinsale.'

*

Mandy Rice Davies owned two restaurants in Tel Aviv, and when one had tried the Georgian Russian restaurant and sampled basic Israeli cooking elsewhere, the discerning digestion directed you to one of hers.

At one side of the patch there was her Chinese restaurant, at the other her European restaurant, Mandy's. She managed to get the food, the atmosphere, and the prices, just right in each of them. Andy Ferguson, Ritter's sometime flatmate, was enjoying dinner with veteran war correspondent James Cameron when the restaurateur approached their table.

'I know you! ...James Cameron?'

Cameron nodded and rose from his chair, extending his hand. 'I have to admit it. And of course, I recognise you, my dear.'

He introduced Ferguson to the one-time call girl who had starred in what had become known as the Profumo Affair, and helped bring down a Conservative government.

'Are you here for the war?'

'Well… we were here for the war, but we've been here long enough, now, without it happening. So we're going back tomorrow after breakfast. Eight o'clock Alitalia flight out of here, a couple of days R and R in Rome, eating decent food, like yours, then back to Blighty.'

'Oh no, Mr Cameron! Don't get the first flight! You'll miss what you came for.'

'Miss what? The bloody war?'

'That's right. It will start tomorrow, before noon.'

Ferguson said: 'They've been saying that since I arrived. *Sempre domani*. Always tomorrow.'

'But this is true! You'll see. Tell you what… why not get the two o'clock? What's the difference? And you see if I'm right.'

'I'll tell you', said Ferguson. 'The two-o'clock doesn't stop at Rome. It's direct to London. No spag. bol. on that flight. And no day off.'

'Well it's up to you. But I think your editors would be upset with you if you left Israel at the precise time the war started.'

'It never works like that,' said Cameron. 'If I miss the first flight, someone will say the war's going to start tomorrow night. If I wait, somebody will tell me the war will start on Tuesday, and so on.'

'Believe me, boys. I know the war will start before noon tomorrow. After all, we're going to start it.'

Cameron raised his eyebrows at that. 'We are?'

Mandy Rice Davies moved closer to Cameron, confidentially: 'My husband works for El Al – and there's a strict rule that no El Al personnel can be called up unless war is imminent. Imminent, here, means within twenty-four hours.'

'And?' Cameron sucked his teeth.

'And he was called up yesterday – at noon.'

'Let's drink to that, then. What would you recommend, my dear? After all, it's your restaurant.'

'The Cabernet is very nice.'

He summoned a waiter: 'Another bottle of Baron Rothschild's best!'

Eli Bogart, walking through the restaurant as though heading for a table, stopped to say hello to Mandy Rice Davies. She introduced him to the two reporters.

'The *Standard*'s famous Mr Cameron! And Mr Ferguson,' he said, shaking hands. 'I believe you're with the London *Post*.'

Ferguson laughed. 'Then you'll believe anything! But you happen to be right.'

Bogart shrugged. 'I work for the Foreign Ministry here... It's my job to know people. You like our local wine?' Bogart asked, when invited to join them in a drink. 'You are quite right in acknowledging it as Rothschild's; the Baron sent his estate manager to organise our vineyards. Nevertheless, despite his best efforts they say it works out at nearly one grape for each bottle!'

The men talked about the war. Bogart agreed that it was 'probably imminent'.

'Tomorrow morning?' Cameron inquired. He caught Mandy's eyes and she shook her head to indicate that he should not reveal his source.

'Tomorrow morning, perhaps,' agreed Bogart. 'Or perhaps the next day.'

They talked about London and mutual friends in Fleet Street. It appeared that Mandy, and Bogart who said he had been stationed there as a diplomat, knew almost as many journalists in London as Cameron and Ferguson. Bogart mentioned Ritter, who, he said, he had once met at an embassy function: 'What a drinker, eh?'

'He says he drinks to make other people appear interesting. Sometimes he says he's just drinking to forget –

trouble is, he can't remember what.' said Ferguson, adding that the two of them shared a flat in Kensington.

'No! Small world! How is he? What's he up to these days?'

'Oh, this and that. Normally – I mean if there actually was a war on here – he'd be jumping on the news editor's desk demanding to be sent out here. As it is, he's on some special story. I've no idea what. He's had nothing in the paper for days.'

'A special, you say? Obviously, then, you can't tell me about that. What was he doing last?'

'I can't tell you, Eli, because I don't know. Last thing he had in the paper was a piece from Ireland. The IRA had been blowing up German-owned farms. Chas did a piece on why they were doing it.'

Shortly afterwards Bogart announced that it was time for him to leave. He went back to his office and telephoned Alitalia, to book a seat on a plane to London via Rome. Much later, Cameron and Ferguson returned to their hotel rooms. They rang Alitalia, too, to cancel their seats on the flight.

*

Monday, June 5, 1967

At seven forty-five, and for the next three hours, the Israeli Air Force, commanded by Major General Mordechai Hod, launched a pre-emptive all-out attack on Arab airfields. Flying in low, under enemy radar screens, they destroyed the Egyptian Air Force. The precise timing was based on the – correct – assumption that the Egyptian pilots would be driving from home to their bases after breakfast, and not on alert with their aircraft.

Later, the Israelis turned on the air forces of Jordan, Syria and Iraq.

Shortly after eight, an Alitalia jet taking off from Tel Aviv was buzzed by Iraqi MiG fighters, which had already strafed Netanya, on the Mediterranean coast. Anxious British journalists who had given up waiting for a war rushed forward to the cockpit and asked the Italian pilot to turn back. Eli Bogart, sitting in the very back row of the plane, was content that the pilot refused.

Andrew Ferguson heard the news on the radio in his room in the Hilton. He tried to phone London but was told that no international lines were available. He also tried to phone Cameron, but the line was permanently engaged.

*

Ted Foxcroft shoved himself out of the encircling leather arms of his 'captain's chair' and stumped across to the sideboard.

'Black or white?'

'White, please – sugar.'

'Damn crazy here now, you know. The Service is going to prohibit the tea clubs and abolish the trolleys, and put bloody vending machines in instead. Oh, and they think the executive dining room should be closed down, too.' He poured two cups of coffee from a percolator, added cream from a carton he had taken from a small fridge built-in to cherry-wood wall cabinets, and carried them back across the salmon-pink carpet. The two senior government intelligence experts sipped quietly.

'I mean, you'd understand if it was the Association, claiming that the tea clubs and the senior dining room were elitist, divisive, that sort of thing. But no: it's the blasted bureaucrats again. Indeed, the Association has told them it's good for morale to leave things as they are – basis for social life and all that. Then what? Bloody paper-clip wallahs reckon that milk bottles are unsightly, that having a civil servant brewing up tea for the chaps in his room is a waste of time. I'll tell you this, it's less a waste of time than the whole blinking lot of them trooping downstairs to some stupid Jap machine on the hour every hour... Coffee all right?'

'Fine, thank you.'

'Kenyan. George, the messenger, gets it and sells it as you need it. Buys it by the ton, I expect, from one of the dingy embassies. Probably pays sod-all for it, and then charges the earth. What the hell, they've all got some sort of fiddle going, as far as I can see. Probably have to pay them twice as much if they hadn't. Let me fill your cup.'

'Thank you; let me help myself.'

'Pass your cup over here. Sometimes I think it's the only exercise I get, these days.'

The Minister, known to Fleet Street tabloids as the 'Spymaster General', watched as Foxcroft again played waiter, then allowed his gaze to survey the room. Three of the walls, the ones without windows, were made up of cherry wood fittings, and each had a door connecting with another office. Built in to the wall facing a modestly-sized leather-top desk with a green shaded light glowing on it was a large-screen television set. If rumour was correct, the TV was an extravagance the hated bureaucrats might get wise to next, for rumour said it was used only for watching the BBC news – he didn't recognise any other source of news apart from the BBC and the *Daily Telegraph* – and sport.

He had survived the parachute drops into France and Holland with a limp – two inches out of his shinbone and a built-up shoe – which had resulted in his being moved from the Airborne Division to what he always described as the 'chairborne division', or VRE, the Very Rear Echelon. The windows of the office, which overlooked St James Park, were double-glazed, one-way vision and (again according to office rumour) made of shell-proof glass: Foxcroft's other leg, the Minister told himself, was therefore relatively safe.

Green roller blinds were fitted on the inside of the windows; there were no curtains. The chairs were all of dark-grained leather, as were the blotters (blue-black blotting paper in front of all the chairs except Foxcroft's which was dark green: Foxcroft used only green ink) placed neatly around a cherry-wood conference table, which could seat twelve. The Minister reckoned that it was, all in all, a suitably impressive office for the head of the Secret Intelligence Service.

'Going to pot then, you might say.'

Foxcroft stared at him, quizzically.

'What is?'

'The civil servant's tea… You could say it was going to pot.'

'You could say that. If you wanted,' said Foxcroft, studiously ignoring the officers' mess humour that he always felt distinguished soldiery from his adopted milieu, The Warbox, as some of its members preferred to be known.

'Anyway, you didn't come here to listen to my bellyaching about tea clubs…'

He reached into a drawer and took out a file, laced into a yellow folder.

'We made a bit of a cock-up in 1945, I'm afraid. Not really anybody's fault, I must say, but a cock-up, nevertheless. The problem was that we were pretty short on the Int. front, so far as the Reds were concerned, in fact we didn't even know how to explain Marxism and Soviet policy…'

'I know; Malcolm Muggeridge told me the only up-to-date information available on what communism was about was a cutting from *The Spectator*. Your lot had it copied and then – would you believe? – marked it Top Secret!'

'Really? I didn't know.'

'It's not surprising,' said the Minister. 'The other day I was shown a letter from the CO of an RAF station telling people to invite all their friends to the airfield's annual dance. Before it left his office it had been stamped Confidential. – But go on.'

'...Well, anyway, in 1945 the only people with up-to-date files on the Russians were the Germans, in fact Gehlen's lot. And we had to strike a deal.'

'We know all this.'

'Yes, of course... And we had to let some go, some who were, in the strictest sense, war criminals.'

'I know...'

'You see, we let a couple of pretty bad war criminals out through the rat-lines – rat-lines that we were running as part of the deal. And it might get out, and rebound on us. Even at this stage.'

'I know... You let Mengele out. And Eichmann too, but he's been recaptured. There's no greater war criminal than those two.'

Foxcroft took a sip of his coffee. He was about to stop this irritating bugger telling him he knew everything: 'I'm afraid it looks as though there was one who was greater.'

As matter-of-factly as he could, Foxcroft explained to the political overlord of Britain's intelligence services about the intended freeing of Morell, the apparent accidental release of the doctor's number-one patient, now dead, and the involvement of the *Post* and Ritter in the search for the grave.

'Nobody's to blame. But it's going to be damned embarrassing if it ever comes out.'

'Embarrassing? I suppose that's one word for it! I think we'd better agree immediately that someone is to blame. Frankly, my money's on you. Or, at least, this office, your predecessors, I mean. The question is, what are we going to do about it?'

'D-Notices, for a start, then I'd like to get this *Post* fellow under wraps.'

'Under wraps? Arrest him, you mean? On what pretext?'

'National security.'

'No. I won't countenance that. Not the arrest of a journalist.'

'Those two journalists were arrested following the Vassal tribunal, and they were jailed.'

'Couldn't be more different. Mulholland and Foster were jailed for refusing to disclose a source, and under a different administration. We wouldn't have done it. Embarrassing a government over something that happened twenty-odd years ago isn't national security. On that basis you couldn't even justify a D-Notice. And if you did, my money would be on the editor ignoring it – he can, you know.'

'Of course it's national security. That's why we don't release cabinet papers for fifty years. It must have occurred to you what mileage the Kremlin will get out of this. And what about our relationship with the Yanks?'

'Russia won't want to make capital out of this. They can't. They've been claiming on the QT that they've got his body and are hanging on to it for safe-keeping. They put it in People's Hospital Number Six, or some other stupidly-named place, for Stalin and his successors to gloat over. What odds will you give me that they're anxious to shout "Oops, our mistake, wrong body"...? And, as for our relations with the Americans, we don't really have any. Not since Harold accused them of bugging Number Ten. Oh, yes, and next month we're altering the fifty-year rule to thirty... Of course, there is a better way of fixing the *Post*.'

'What's that?'

'Co-operate with them.'

'We can't do that!'

'Oh I don't know. I can. I'll speak to Porter. I'll get him round now. Leave it with me.'

He stood up to leave. 'By the way, if you were to put a precise date on this cock-up, as you call it, which month did it occur?'

'Round about the middle.'

'May-June, you mean?'

'That's right.'

'That's OK, then,' said the Minister, with a smile, and walked out of the room.

*

'You bastard! You stupid bastard!' screeched Porter as he and Morris waited on the pavement for the office car to pull across Whitehall from its parking spot. 'Do you realise that you could have had us jailed, for that?'

'For what?'

'For refusing to disclose information, of course, you fool! Why did you tell the Minister you didn't know where Morell is?'

'Because I don't know.'

'Don't lie to me as well, or you can go back and clear your fucking desk now.'

'Bugger me, cock! You threatening to fire me? You can stick your job up your arse... I don't know where Morell is, and I don't know where Ritter is. I honestly don't, I wasn't lying.'

'Why haven't you asked McKeown?'

'He doesn't know, either.'

'I don't believe this! We've got one of our top reporters running about somewhere in Ireland, and nobody knows where? Why doesn't Bill McKeown know?'

'Because he doesn't want to. That's the sort of professional he is. If he doesn't know, then you and I don't know. That way, you don't get sent to jail for failing to reveal what nobody knows. You should be grateful your people look after you so well.'

'I put you in charge of this. But I'm the fucker who goes to jail. Do you understand that? So you'd better find out exactly where Ritter is.'

'Bugger me! You're not fucking listening to me, are you? So I do that... Then what? What if I find out? What do I do if the Minister asks me again?'

'Tell him, I suppose. Oh, shit...! I don't know. Do whatever you like. But I am not going to jail for you or for that long streak of Tyneside shit, Ritter.'

*

At noon in Fleet Street, McKeown was trying to raise Ferguson. He was too preoccupied to register the sight of the editor and managing editor walking together into the newsroom.

'There's a chap on the line who says he's a friend of Ritter's, but won't give his name,' said Monica, the news desk secretary.

'Put him over to me,' McKeown told his secretary. '...Hello, can I help you?'

'Are you Chas Ritter's boss?'

'He might disagree, but, sometimes, I think I am.'

'Look, I don't know what job he's on, I don't want to. But when you speak to him next tell him there's another bloke here looking for him. This one's of sort of Wild West extraction, he'll know what I mean. Driving a grey Triumph 2000. Tell him the piano player rang. Cheers.'

NINE

'What would you like to be done with the grave?'

'I'm sorry; I don't understand.'

'The way I see it, you are the nearest thing to a next of kin as far as this grave's concerned. What do you want me to do about it?'

Doctor Morell shook his head. 'I tell you: there is no grave. This is nothing to do with me.'

'You see,' Ritter explained, 'What we are going to do is photograph the grave, whichever one it is. Then it will be splashed all over the *Post*'s front page, half-page pictures on page three, acres of writing, nothing else at all in the paper to speak of. It will be on the news on radio and TV the night before our paper hits the streets. It will then be on the radio all the next day, in all the evening papers around the world, and all the world's radio stations, the next day and every day for weeks. It will be in every newspaper in the world that your beloved Führer didn't die in Berlin and that we have found Hitler's actual grave. This village won't know what's hit it. You won't be able to get a car into the place. Extra policemen will be drafted in just to direct traffic; the *Gardai* will be buying new homes on the basis of the overtime they'll be pulling in. There'll be reporters and photographers climbing trees and peering through every letter box in the street. They'll pay people to talk to them, whatever they have to say. Even if they have nothing to say. The television camera teams will use so much power that all the lights will go out. It will be chaos. The only people who might gain are Mrs Brown, with her shop, and Maire at the Badgers. But they'll both run out of fags and booze before teatime on the first day. Your only hope, yours and Mrs Morell's, is that you cooperate a bit more and then we'll put you up in an hotel somewhere safe, totally at our expense, until all the fuss has died down. Then you can come home. Of course, at some stage, hopefully some time before everybody else arrives, we'll have to have the grave dug up and the contents taken away for examination and identification. The opening of the grave will be a major world event, part of European history. Even if we open it in private we'll have to film it, for posterity. So... what I thought you might like to do is help us by telling us which grave it is and talking it through. Is it Kelleher?...'

Ritter studied Morell's pale round face hoping for a sign of emotion.

'Or is it Cully?... Look... Doctor Morell, it seems to me that the best way through this is to do it civilly. Tell me which grave – you know it's only a matter of time before I find out – and then we'll do it properly. My paper will get somebody from the appropriate authority, I don't know what, it could be something like the Imperial War Museum, or anything, and they will very quietly open the grave and take the thing away. You can be assured that it will be properly handled, treated with respect, if that's what's worrying you. You know it makes sense. Meanwhile, we'll spirit you and Mrs Morell out of the way while the Fleet Street heavy mobs and rat packs come clumping through town.'

'You cannot do this,' said Morell. 'There can be no grave robbing, I have told you there is no grave to rob, there can be no bringing of the world press, I forbid it.'

'Well, doctor, you can forbid all you like. I'll see you after lunch.'

But when Ritter next knocked on the doctor's door after his now-daily Guinness and stew, Mrs Morell told him her husband was unable to see him.

'I think you were unkind to him this morning. Too unkind. He has had to go to bed to rest. Why are you like this to him? He thought he had given you a story. He is not a young man any longer, you know, and his heart has never been strong.'

'I'm sorry, Mrs Morell, I really am. But I can't leave it here. I can't offer my paper only half a story when the other half is so close. Let your husband stay in bed this afternoon, and we'll have another chat tomorrow.' The doctor could be left to simmer; he had other things to do.

A bemused Maire at the Badgers had told Ritter that the nearest undertaker was twenty miles away. She laughed. 'Why do you want to know? You're not worried about my lamb stew?'

Ritter, who thought his backside could be welded to a car seat, decided it was a good day for a drive.

*

'You're English?' asked the undertaker. He stepped behind his bench and looked out of the dusty window at the 1100. 'But you drive a car with an Irish registration. Doesn't look like one of them hire cars.'

'Borrowed it from a friend.'

'Fair enough.' He removed a cigarette from behind his ear, and examined it. It was still burning. He wet his fingers and tamped it out. He took another from a Gallagher's packet in the pouch of his apron, lighted it, drew on it heavily and assumed a thoughtful pose.

'Well, of course,' he said, after waiting until he was exactly half-way down the cigarette, 'I keep all the coffins in my book.' He creased his eyes against the sawdust, which floated across shafts of light streaming through the window. 'I suppose I can look in the book. Why exactly do you want to know?'

'I thought of writing a little book about the church,' lied Ritter. 'But I thought I should know about all the people who are buried there.'

'It's not much of a place to write a book about. It's not even big enough to write home about, if you ask me. Still... I

suppose that's your concern. Didn't you ask the priest? That
would be Father Dennis.'

'These two were just before his time.'

He opened his ledger. 'Course, I don't necessarily do
everything that you in England might call funeral directing. I
just do the coffins, mainly.'

He ran his nicotine-stained thumb down the red ink
columns of neat handwriting. 'Ah! Kelleher, here he is. Died
just over twenty years ago, August 1945, this the one?'

'How old was he?'

'Now why would I know that? With some people you get
given the date of birth, but all that matters to me is that he
won't get any older.'

'Did he have any next of kin?'

'Not any who wanted to pay for the burial. Father
O'Toole looked after that.'

'Do you know anything about him?'

'Well, it was a six foot coffin, so he'd be less than six feet
tall.'

'Most people are. Can you remember what he looked
like?'

'I never saw him. I built the coffin. Somebody in the
village would do the laying out, you know, preparing the
body for viewing. I told you, it's not like English
undertakings, here. You don't need a chapel of rest, as they
style it, so much here: people are quite happy to lay out in
their own front parlours. Let's see, now... and Cully, another
one booked by Father O'Toole – though there's nothing
strange in itself about that. This one was paid for from
abroad, as I remember it, because I recall it took more than a
week to get the bank to exchange it into punts. It was a
money order. Spanish? Something like that. What do they
use? Lira, escudos, pesetas? I don't know. Some such things
as that.'

'Is there no way of finding out what it was?'

'Not now, I doubt even the bank would remember. This was, let's see, yes, back end of '45.'

'You didn't lay him out, either?'

'No. But he was a six-foot coffin, too. And now you know as much as myself.'

Ritter did not need to order his purchases when he went in to Mrs Brown's shop. Either Mrs Brown would be there or, if her arthritis was playing her up, her young assistant, the delightful Deirdre, would be serving. Whichever it was, they knew what the reporter would ask for.

'Two Wrigley's and two Polos, Mr Ritter? Here you are.'

The lovely Deirdre handed him the change out of half-a-crown. Ritter studied her. She was without doubt the most attractive female in the village, slightly taller than average with definitively Titian bright golden auburn hair tumbling in pre-Raphaelite curls to rest on her perfectly shaped breasts. During an earlier purchase he had established that she was eighteen.

Ritter nodded towards the ceiling. 'Arthritis again?'

When she eventually appeared Mrs Brown walked painfully behind Deirdre and crossed to the window. She took a folded napkin and placed it over the clock which the Morell's used as their timekeeper, and walked slowly back to the stairs. She hadn't spoken to Deirdre, and she hadn't even seen Ritter, who was obscured from her view by a rotary display of paperback books he was inspecting.

'She did that the other day,' said Ritter when she had disappeared. 'Why does she do it?'

'I don't know. I've never asked her. I used to think that it was to protect it from the sun, but she sometimes does it when it's cloudy. Perhaps it used to be because of the sun. I think that she does it now mainly because she's always done it. You know, she is an old lady. She has these habits.'

'It must be annoying for the Morells over the road.' said Ritter. 'They haven't got a clock anywhere in their house, so they use yours, the one in the window, to tell the time. When

Mrs Brown covers the clock face they can't tell what time it is.'

'I never knew that!' said Deirdre. 'That's the strangest thing I ever heard. And the Morells are more or less her only friends, too.'

'Speak of the devil,' said Ritter, as the tiny copper bell tinkled above the shop door as it opened to admit Doctor Morell.

'Afternoon, doctor.' Morell looked put out to find Ritter standing there. The relationship between the two men had cooled with the reporter's persistent questioning about the graveyard. He looked around the shop as if unsure what he had come to buy.

Ritter said: 'Give him a loaf of bread.'

He wished Deirdre and Morell cheerio and walked through the still open door into the street. He was not surprised to see the doctor removing the cloth covering from the clock. He waited for a few minutes, but Morell did not reappear. He was clearly undecided about his other purchases.

*

Mary-Rose Morrissey said that she always did the laying out, unless people died in hospital, or had post mortems there, in which case they were collected by the undertaker and delivered, already prepared, for wake and burial.

'Kelleher, I remember, died in his sleep, he was an old man, you know. Cully, had a heart attack, I think, he was old, too. You know, when people are, well, expected to die anyway, there's no need for a post mortem, or an inquest. You just get a death certificate and that's it.'

'Can you remember what they were like, Kelleher and Cully?'

'I didn't really know them, not either of them. I don't know... average height, five foot six or seven, grey hair – you know: old men.'

'How long had they lived in the village?'

'Not long, I think, the pair of them. I'm not sure, but they probably came around the end of the war, perhaps nineteen forty-five or forty six. I know that Mr Kelleher hadn't actually lived here very long at all when he died.'

'In 1945, when Mr Kelleher died, you say he was an old man? How old would you say?'

'Oh, Mr Ritter, I don't know. It was twenty years ago. I was twenty years younger. Maybe he just looked old. He could have been anything.... Not old, really, but I don't know, he'd been ill, and whatever he'd had, he died from it.'

'You said he died in his sleep.'

'Yes, I think he did. Most people do, you know. Not always in bed, sometimes in an armchair or something. They feel tired, they sit down, and then they might die. That's the most common way to die, I reckon, unless it's an accident, of course.'

'Could Mr Kelleher, do you think, have been as young as, say, er –' Ritter pretended to be plucking a figure out of the air – 'er, fifty-six?'

'Ooh, I wouldn't think so, I'm not normally so bad on ages. But, I don't know, I couldn't say yes or no to be honest. Anyway, he wouldn't be younger than fifty-six... Well, he could have been fifty-six, if I think about it.'

'And Cully? Could he have been about the same age?'

'Are you going to put this in the paper? I don't really want to say anything that might be wrong.'

'No, nothing like that. At least, if I was, I'd make sure it was right first. I might put it in a book.'

'Well, he could have been. But don't forget, he'd been ill. They'd both been ill. I don't know, I suppose he could have been, but he looked older.'

'So neither of them was really that old?'

'Well, you see, I seem to remember them as being old, I mean grey, and frail-looking. But now you mention it, they might not have been that old.' She smoothed out a non-existent crease in her pinafore. 'Point is, as I say, I was twenty years younger myself, then. What I thought of as being old in those days might not look so old when I'm a bit nearer that age myself. You know, when you're at school, you think your parents are ancient, then suddenly, you are at whatever age they were, and it doesn't seem so old at all. So I can't honestly say with these two. Mind you, they died. They were old enough to die naturally.'

'But when you saw them, they were dead. I suppose dead people do look a bit older. When they were alive, do you still remember that they looked old?'

'I don't know, really. Mr Cully, I think, had a sort of limp, as if he'd been injured on one side. It might have been during the war, perhaps. But I don't recall him having any scars, as such, although he was sort of pock-marked down his back, as if he'd once been hit by – oh, I don't know – shotgun pellets, that sort of thing. Not, mark you, that I've ever seen shotgun wounds, not outside looking at a rabbit, but that's how I imagine it. Mr Kelleher was definitely older-looking than him when he died. He was sort of stooped, I think. But I think they both were.'

'Just one thing; there'd have been death certificates, wouldn't there – who would have signed those?'

'Doctor Dalrymple, I suppose. Of course, he's dead too, now.'

Deirdre was coming out of Mrs Brown's shop as Ritter walked back towards the Badgers from Mary-Rose Morrissey's home. He stopped to talk while she busied herself with several keys required to lock the door for the night.

He urgently needed to celebrate. He had cracked the story of the decade, the best story since the war. Hitler had escaped to Ireland, and lived under an assumed name. Cully. When he died, the other Nazis, who had escaped with him – the money would have come from South America, more likely than from Spain, but maybe it would come via Spain – paid for his burial. Obviously they'd be tipped off by Doctor Morell, and asked to contribute to a whip-round. It was all there, the injury down one side, the pock-marks on his back from the oak splinters, the foreign currency. Shit! He couldn't wait to see the old quack's face when he confronted him! But he'd leave it until morning. And then he'd cross the street to make a triumphant call to McKeown. He'd be chuffed. This would cause a Kinnell or two and a bit of spectacle biting. He would have to get the team up and running. But right now he needed to celebrate, and there was nobody with whom he would rather celebrate than the gorgeous Deirdre.

'Do you ever go down the Badgers? Would you like to come in for a drink?'

'It's a lovely day, and still warm out. And you're a city man, I realise, so why not come for a walk? Tell you what, we'll get the best of both worlds and walk over the top to the next village and have a drink there.'

As they crossed the road Ritter put his hand in the small of her back, as if to guide her through the traffic. There was no traffic, but at least he had made contact. They left the road at the church and walked behind it following a footpath, which stretched up a grassy hill. There were rabbits playing in the heather, unaffected by the close proximity of humans. He put his arm around her, to help point her in their direction. There was no hint of resistance; it felt good.

'They're like my rabbits,' said Ritter, 'At home. Or at what used to be home.'

'You had your own rabbits? Pet rabbits, you mean?'

'My garden, when I lived in Northumberland, would be ankle deep in rabbits in the morning and early evening. They were too close together, even, for me to be able to shoot them.'

'So you used not to be a townie, then?'

'I was born in a city, but brought up in the countryside, on Tyneside. Newcastle is a town, or rather a city, true enough. But if you walk a couple of hundred yards north of Marks and Spencer's you fall off the edge. They've just built a civic centre, what people used to call a town hall, and across the road there's green fields. It's not really like living in a city – the sea is only ten miles away, at the end of the Tyne, and I can't think that anywhere in Newcastle is more than a mile or so from the river; of course, if it's so far from the river it's closer to the country, so everybody grows up either with the river or the greenery on their doorstep.'

They had reached a makeshift stile, not more than a gap in a wall, but arranged with steps so that sheep couldn't make their way through it. Ritter climbed through first, then held out his hand for Deirdre. She took it, and jumped down to the grass. She didn't let go of his hand when she landed.

'Where I lived we had both river and countryside,' he continued; 'the buildings thinned out so much that I had the river at the front door and the country at the back. Mind you, the fishing wasn't much, but we would have deer coming into the garden, and usually a fox or two.'

'Gracious, I hope you didn't go after shooting the deer like you did the rabbits! Why did you ever leave such a place for London? I've never been, but it can't be anything to compare.'

'I had a wife. I still do, sort of. I had a great job and I needed to go to London to make it even greater, because that's where the stories are, or at least, it's where they start. She had horses, and when I wanted to move she had to choose between the horses and me. She chose the horses. So she lives in what used to be the marital home, with Dobbin, her horse, and I share a cellar – a basement flat – with a half-Scottish, half-Italian reporter – what the Scots call a Tally.'

When they reached the pub at the other side of the hill Ritter asked for a bottle of Champagne, even specifying 'vintage', but all he got was an old-fashioned look from the landlord, so he settled for a pint of Guinness for himself and Babycham for Deirdre, and they took them outside so they could sit on the fence of the pub's yard and wait for the sunset.

'In your job, do you meet a lot of interesting people? Famous, I mean. I bet you must.'

'I suppose I do, really,' said Ritter. 'Or at least I used to. I worked for a while at London Airport, covering all the famous people and the VIPs who travelled. If you go almost anywhere in the world you have to go via LAP, as we called it, so I met people who were not even necessarily coming to London, but just passing through. When I was there, a few years ago, I met just about everybody in the world who was famous. Sophia Loren and David Niven, Richard Burton and Elizabeth Taylor, Katharine Hepburn and Spencer Tracy, Cassius Clay, everybody in the Royal Family... I used to send my wife – she was my girlfriend, then – a post card every day. I'd just put: "Today I interviewed..." then a list of names, Lord Mountbatten, Bing Crosby – he and his wife had just been to the St Leger and were flying to Ireland – Marlene Dietrich, Sean Connery, Margot Fonteyn, Ella Fitzgerald, Nat King Cole...'

'Did you meet the Beatles?'

'Meet 'em? I toured with them for a month.'

'What were they like?'

'Very funny. What I remember most, apart from all the girls screaming, was laughing 'til my sides ached.'

'And the Rolling Stones?'

'I toured with them, too. I was one of the younger reporters on the paper. It was the sort of thing the young 'uns always had to do.'

'Were they very dirty, the Rolling Stones? Their hair always looked dirty.'

'I suppose it must've looked it, because everybody says that. But it wasn't dirty, it was just long. You know, when the Beatles started everybody thought their hair was long. It was, for the time. I asked John Lennon once, did he mind people copying him by wearing Beatle wigs? He said: 'They're not copying us – we don't wear Beatle wigs!'

He gave her his line about possibly working on a book about the village, and told her another of his favourite Beatle stories: how a guy called Barry Norman, a show-biz writer on the *Mail*, had asked the Beatles what they thought they would be doing in five years' time, and Paul McCartney had replied: 'Much the same', then defensively asked: ' – what will you be doing?' Norman had replied that he was writing a book about Edward Lear, and fancied it would be in paperback by then. And how, next morning, Lennon had shown Ritter the draft lyrics for a new hit, *Paperback Writer*.

'I see why you like your job. I bet there were a lot of girls when you were doing those pop tours.' She was looking at him, through her hair, which shone like gold in the evening sunshine.

'There were lots of young girls, and some not so young, who wanted to go backstage. They'd write letters saying "I'll do anything" – underlined three times – "to meet the Beatles" or whoever. I think they meant it. But what they wanted was to do it with the group, not with some reporter. The fact of the matter was that the days were spent travelling and the nights watching the shows and filing your copy – phoning your stories to the paper – then trying to get out of town with the lads without too much hassle. It didn't leave a lot of time for a personal life, or even for a sex life, despite what they say in the Sunday papers.'

'And do you have a girl friend in London, now?'

'Not a special one. I'm hardly ever there. I've been right round the world in the last twelve months; in fact I was abroad five months of the year, last year. It's very handy for tax reasons, but plays hell with any romances.'

'Your wife maybe made the right decision, then?'

'She'd say so. Perhaps if we'd both moved to London I'd have travelled less.'

'But no horses, no foxes, no rabbits, no deer.'

'That's what they call quality of life. But there'd be no fun for me, or not much, either. And not so many good jobs. You have to do that while you're young enough. The good life will still be there when I'm older.'

'You talk as if time was running out.'

'Deirdre, my love, as Benjamin Franklin said, "nothing's certain, except death and taxes". You can't run away from either of them.'

'But Frederick the Great said, "You dogs, would you live for ever?" And anyway, Franklin also said that at twenty years of age the will reigns; at thirty, the wit; and at forty the judgment. So maybe when judgment prevails you'll go back to real life.'

'There is that. Whatever Fleet Street is, it isn't real life.' He turned towards her. 'Where did you read Frederick the Great, and Franklin? At school?'

'In the shop, at home, in bed... in a book of quotations. Actually they're on the same page. Frederick and Franklin.' she pointed down the grassy slope to where the village lay. 'There's not much else to do. I don't have a regular boy friend either. It's not because I travel the world though. There's nobody here. True, if I go to Dublin, there's boys to dance with, to court you even, but nobody for real. I suppose that when I want to wed I'll just up and go to Dublin, or London maybe, and find someone.'

Deirdre's parents, she told Ritter, were both dead. She lived in what had been the family home with her elder sister and her husband. It was clear that she didn't like her brother in law, who was unemployed, but played guitar in a rock and roll group.

After three more pints for Ritter and two gins for Deirdre, they started back. The sky was deep purple. On the summit they sat on a rock and watched it darken further.

Ritter sat and thought. He had a great story in his notebook, and a magnificent-looking girl at his side. 'At times like this,' he told her, 'I know that there is a god.'

He felt Deirdre shiver with the oncoming night cold. He put his arm more tightly around her shoulders, and then rubbed her back, as if to make her warmer. He felt her bra strap and wondered why men always wanted to feel a bra strap, even – perhaps especially – through clothing; they knew when a woman was wearing one, so why the need to confirm it? It wasn't as though it was sexy. Or wasn't it?

'You know,' he told her, 'you're beautiful. Give us a kiss.'

'I thought you'd never ask,' said Deirdre as she folded into Ritter's arms. His right hand cupped her right breast.

'Do you like big breasts? I'm a thirty-eight-and-a-half. And,' she added proudly, covering his hand with hers, 'I've got a very narrow back.' She took his forefinger and traced it around one of the buttons on her blouse. Then she poked the finger through a gap between the buttons, and into her cleavage, and placed her open mouth over his.

Ritter quickly unbuttoned her, and unhooked her bra, tumbling her hard smooth breasts into his hands.

'I'm a virgin,' Deirdre told him. 'Well, sort of. But I'm ready to lose it now…'

He kissed her hardening nipples and ran his hands through her beautiful hair. She parted her legs and squeezed his leg between the top of hers, pressing her pelvic bone hard against him. 'I'd like to do it with you, Charles.'

'I want to do it, too, sweetheart. I really do. But when we do it, for your first time, it will be in a comfortable bed.' He hooked and buttoned her up, kissed her again on the mouth, then on the forehead. They stood up, and wiped the grass off their clothes. 'Anyway,' he said with a smile, 'how do you become a "sort of" virgin?'

Deirdre stared at the ground. 'I did it once. But not properly. With my mouth. With my brother-in-law. My sister was away and he was drunk, and he was definitely going to do it one way or another. But Charles, you musn't tell anybody. It would kill my sister!'

*

Ritter didn't get to his own bed until the early hours of the morning. He walked Deirdre back to her sister's home, kissed her goodnight, and took himself back towards the Badgers. The pub was still open – the actual opening hours depended as much on the mood of Maire and her customers as it did on the clock – and by the light from the lounge windows Ritter spotted two familiar shapes: parked in front of the borrowed 1100, half on, half off, the pavement, was a German-registered Audi; and sitting quietly and alone on the bus stop's wooden bench was a German assistant editor, Bayer.

It would have been pointless to try to avoid him by going around to the pub's back door. In any case, Bayer had absolutely traced him and had probably already watched his approach.

'Fuck my old boots – it's Hermann the German! Bayer, you old bastard! What are you doing here?'

'Waiting for you, my friend – for you to finish your walking out with young ladies. All work and no play makes Charles a dull boy, I think. And all sitting and no drinking makes Hermann dull also. Shall we step inside, old chap, for a drink? They are still serving beer inside.'

'How could a man refuse?'

Maire started to pull Ritter's pint as he walked through the door. She nodded in Bayer's direction. 'He found you, then.'

'I found him, actually. He was sitting outside the door, looking like one wise monkey. Better make it two pints.'

He shoved the first pint along the bar towards Bayer. 'Try this. It's as pure as any of your Bavarian beer. Purer.' The German held the pint up to the light. Ritter laughed. 'You'll never see through that stuff.'

'It is a peasouper.'

Ritter thought: *Erbsensuppe*. Same expression. 'In English, that's a fog,' he said.

'Same thing in German, you cannot see through it.'

'In London we'd call it a London particular. At least, that's what Sherlock Holmes would have called it. Just don't let the landlady hear you calling her beer that.' Bayer savoured the expression, and savoured the stout. He would look for an opportunity to work London particular into a sentence.

They took the beers across to an empty corner table and sat down.

'OK, then. How did you find me?'

'You know, Charles, I often think it's a pity that you write off all German journalists simply as stupid, lying, kraut wankers. I found you really easily. I went to the Irish tourist board and asked for lists of all their hotels and pensions. Then I went back to our London bureau and started to telephone. Each number I rang, I said: "Please can I speak to Mr Ritter, it's urgent." I was counting on the hotel remembering your name; it is not common, even if you had left. And of course a journalist makes a lot of use of a telephone. Only this place, the Badgers, said you were not here at the moment but were expected back. It was just old-fashioned thorough reporting. What I expect you, rather pompously, would call Fleet Street style, I do not doubt it. But we stupid krauts can do it, too.'

'Did you ring the Gresham?'

'What's that?'

'It's an hotel in Dublin where I stayed a while ago. Did they say they'd had a guest called Ritter?'

'My dear Charles! I had not even started to ring places in Dublin. I thought it unlikely that Hitler's personal doctor would be living in hiding in the middle of a European capital city. I suppose it was possible, but I thought also that if you had been hiding him in an hotel you would have been outside of a town under an assumed name. My guesswork was that you were interviewing him, and living nearby, under your own name. And I was right, eh?'

'You're talking, wittering on, about Morell, are you? Don't you remember, Hermann? You told me he was dead.'

'I was wrong. I have worked it out. He is alive, and he is living in Ireland. Living here, in fact.'

'How do you figure that?'

'Because you are working on Morell. And you are in Ireland. Oh, and because there is a man living across the street from here called Morell. Is that sufficiently convincing?'

'But how did you know I was here, in the first place.'

'Detective work, Charles! Your car! When I saw you on Friday you had the Irish morning papers on your back seat.'

'I could have bought them in London.'

'Not, I think, the last editions. And not, I think, the Irish edition of the *Daily Mirror*, the one they are experimenting with printing in colour. Experimenting! At *Bild* they are doing it all the time, and they sell more copies!'

Ritter couldn't resist saying: 'But the colour's crap. And the stories are crappier!'

'Sometimes you are right. When you make unjournalistic generalisations, you are always wrong. There's a generalisation for you. Anyway, the Irish papers and the colour Mirror were good clues. Worth the effort, as it turned out, of a few phone calls. Not many; the Badgers, fortunately, comes early in the alphabet.'

'So how do you come up with Morell's being alive? That would be a great story, Hermann.'

'There, I'll bow to you. I remember you saying once, very late at night in some bar somewhere, that a bad investigative reporter starts with what he believes to be true and works out from that, while a good one starts on the outside and works towards the centre to establish the truth of the first factor.'

'Did I say that? I remember a fraud squad superintendent telling me the only way to approach a balance sheet is to assume every item on it is false, then you find the crookery. Same thing, I suppose... Sorry – go on.'

'Belief number one was that Morell was dead and every other factor depended on that. But who said he was dead? Only Axmann, and he wasn't sure. So I started on the outside – literally on the perimeter of the spider's web, *die Spinne* – and traced it all back. Start with the assumption that Morell is alive... and you do not find him dead. In fact you find that Morell lived for a time – you'll like the irony of this – he moved from the bunker to living in a convent in Rome.'

'I know, Siciliana.'

'You've done your footwork well then, Charles. Well done. And you will know then about a Red Cross passport number 108180.'

'101080.'

'Whatever. I was not of course quoting from my notebook. When we were in Hamburg and you thanked me for my help you said I'd be the first to know if your Morell story stood up, or anything developed. Incidentally, you also said you would pay me for my help, but no cheque has arrived. And since then I have given you more help.'

'I'm sorry about the money. You wouldn't know, but we're the slowest payers in the western world. But look, Hermann, the point is this. Morell is, as we now know, I 'fess up, alive and well and living in Ireland. But he's an old man; his memory's not so good. He's not sure about his facts, about details. He contradicts himself. He romances about his own importance and he prattles on about his paranoia over all other doctors. Jesus, the other day he was claiming to have discovered penicillin!'

'He's probably right. At least, partly. A lot of doctors were on the verge of something similar in the early stages of the war. Morell had something like penicillin that he used in the bunker. When it was actually discovered, he thought it was a development of his own idea that had been stolen, that's all. But Charles, the story here, forgive me, is not Theo Morell, scientist, but the last days in the bunker, along with what was wrong with Hitler – was he man or superman? Was Morell slowly killing him, or was he keeping him alive? Did he crap like a mere mortal? Was he screwing Eve Braun? Did he, as is widely believed, have the pox? Did he suffer from –' Bayer's brow creased as he sought for the word – 'Did he suffer from piles?'

'I can tell you something about the pox. Piles, by the way, no he didn't. But everybody thinks that people who behave like him must have congenital syphilis. Henry the Eighth had it apparently. But Hitler didn't. At least, there were routine VD tests – Wasserman, gonorrhoea, that sort of thing, in 1940, and they were all negative. According to our medical editor that means he was pox free. At least he was then. I can't see that he'd have had much opportunity after that. At any rate, it means that syph hadn't made him the way he was. As for crapping, of course he did. Morell used to send it away for analysis.'

'What did it find, Charles? Our readers are very interested in medical stories,' he laughed '– all about that sort of shit.'

'So are ours. In fact the medical editor's the only one who can get his name in the paper six days a week. Well, the only one apart from the chairman.'

They ordered more drink.

'Look. Hermann, I'll level with you. I'll tell you all Morell has told me – I've got notebooks full of it – about the bunker and the medical history, everything you need – on three conditions.'

'Fine. I expect I will agree, whatever they are.'

'The first is that you don't tell your office where we are – even for photographers. In any case, we'll give you pictures when we take them. You haven't told Hamburg where you are, have you?'

'Only that I'm in Ireland, looking for you.'

'We can live with that. Let them think you're still looking. I don't think any other journalist will find us like you did. By the way, congratulations on that.'

The German shrugged.

'Two: you don't interview, or even approach, Doctor Morell until I'm finished with him.'

'Can't I sit in with you on the interview?

'No. It's going too well. It would interrupt the flow.'

'What if I agree not to speak at all?'

'Not even then. The point is that he believes nobody at all knows his whereabouts. Even my boss doesn't know. He'll be mortified if he thinks there's been a leak, even to a German. Maybe especially to a German. I don't want to do anything that might interfere with the rapport that we've established between us.'

'OK. Except that, if the situation changes and if you think that he might be, shall we say, amenable to the suggestion, you will put it to him.'

'Yes,' said Ritter. 'Of course.'

'And three? The third condition?' This would be the trickiest.

'That when I give you the story, your lot gives the *Post* a twenty-four hour start on running it.'

'No, Charles! The deal has to be that we publish together! I have done a lot of work...'

'For God's sake, Hermann. I've done all the work. I've offered you all my notes for nothing. We've put a lot into this. All you've invested is the cost of a few phone calls, plus a ferry ticket. It's my story!'

'But I know it too.'

'But you haven't got it.'

'I could knock on his door and ask him for it, like you did.'

'If you did that he'd stop talking for ever. To anybody. Then you'll have nothing.'

'I'll have as much as you.'

'No you won't. It's the whole deal, or nothing. Look, Hermann, when we publish, the story will make news. It will be in the German press that Morell is talking to the *Post*. But on that same day your lot will announce that he's also talking to you, and that you have an exclusive story. And you'll have the whole lot. We can only run so much each day, but we'll syndicate it world wide. Only, the first day for everybody else is that we have got the story. I will fix it with my lot that you have exclusive first rights in Germany, and for free. If we do day one on the bunker, I will give you the extra stuff that we don't use on the bunker, same when we do it on the medical angle and so on. We'll probably be more interested than you in his escape...'

Ritter was trying to ensure that he made no mention of the fact that Hitler had also escaped. Bayer was excited about the story of finding Morell – he had no idea that there was an even better story, and that Ritter had it in his head and in his notebook. It was possible that Bayer knew about Hitler's escape and was in turn thinking he was holding out on him... but he was never going to trace the story down to a leader of the Third Reich living in hiding under the name of Cully.

That was a *Post* exclusive. Sorry: world exclusive.

'By the way, you probably didn't know that our secret intelligence service, MI6, was instrumental in running Odessa and *die Spinne*.'

'I realised it had to be somebody like that, helping the Nazis, but I didn't know who. Do you have proof of this?'

'Only Morell's word. But that's good enough for us. It's of no interest to him to lie about it. The other thing is that they, MI6, have got somebody looking for Morell. Or at least, for me, which is the same thing. I can tell you about that, as well, but only if you agree to all three conditions.'

'It looks a pretty good package to me, Charles. I know I'll be crucified for agreeing, when I get back to Hamburg. At least, until they see it in print in our paper, then all will be forgotten.' He signalled for more beer. 'OK. I agree.'

'Well, I'm shattered,' said Ritter. Maire was making last orders signals around the pub. 'One drink to celebrate the deal and your share in a world scoop, then I'm off to kip. We'll start the story in the morning. I promise, that by the end of this, you will not be disappointed, and your bosses will be as happy as pigs in shit.'

Bayer collected and paid for the drinks.

'By the way, where are you sleeping?'

'There's no room at the inn for this weary traveller. Unless you can put me up on your floor I shall sleep in my car.'

'Your car it is, then. It's a tough life, isn't it, this international journalism? Cheers.'

TEN

Lough Leane, at 4,500 acres the largest of Killarney's famous lakes, is noted by anglers for its trout and salmon just as much as by tourists who come by car for its scenic beauty. The salmon fishing season runs from January to September, and it's not unusual for half a dozen to be taken on the first day of the season. But the best of it ends in June and, since that is the warmest of the good months, it was the time chosen by Pat Cooney for his annual fishing fortnight. He had a small room in a handy angler's pub that served a healthy breakfast – your own brown trout, if you'd landed a nice half-pounder – and a decent dinner after the full day's casting.

It wasn't the sort of place that English people knew about, but it was the place where Cooney, unpacking, had found Ritter's postcard in his pocket and had put it in the village letterbox.

'I've no idea who those two are,' the landlord told Cooney, nodding towards two English men who sat shielding the fire from the rest of the taproom. 'I could have sworn that when they arrived they had no rods with them. And the stuff that they've got is surely brand new.'

'We were all beginners, once,' said Cooney, philosophically.

'To be sure, Pat. But have you ever heard tell of a fishing man asking a fishing pub if it served lunch?'

'Lunch? You mean, at dinner time?'

'While the wife was serving them their supper, they asked what time was lunch.'

'Lunch, here in a fishing pub? You never know for sure, like; maybe they're expecting rain.'

It was a good joke. The landlord laughed with Cooney. 'Sure now, the more you look at 'em, the more I see you've got it. They look the types afraid of getting a wee bit wet.' 'You know what I think?' offered Cooney. 'I think you should keep your eye on them. They're fishy, that's what they are.'

The landlord was sufficiently amused to buy his guest a small Bushmills.

*

Without any doubt, said Kerrigan, it was the best assignment the *Post* had ever offered him. Bill McKeown had rung and told him and Connolly to head for Kinsale and book in to a decent hotel and wait for further instructions. The two reporters hadn't waited to be told twice: news editors had a habit of changing their minds if they thought they might be giving you a job that could be pleasant. He'd told them to book Foley, the freelance, to cover for them on a daily rate until further notice. The only information he could tell them, and which they could tell Foley if necessary – it's better if a freelance feels you trust him enough to confide your office information – was that the job was a baby-sit.

'We'll book in under false names, then,' Kerrigan had suggested, getting the taste for a spot of adventure. Cloak and dagger jobs, or even run-of-the-mill buy-ups, rarely came the way of Dublin office.

'For God's sake, no!' McKeown had screamed down the phone. 'Use your own names. False names are far too complicated. In any case, I don't mind people in Kinsale knowing you're about, it won't do the *Post*'s image any harm for you to be seen in a couple of decent restaurants round that way, especially during the Irish drive. Get a pretty good hotel, not a doss house. And give your wives the phone numbers and forwarding address, just in case. Get settled in, then await further instructions.'

Connolly concurred: it was the best assignment. He interpreted the instructions simply as to book in to the best hotel in Kinsale with carte blanche at every restaurant. And Kinsale certainly had some to choose from. They were not likely to get a better assignment in Connolly's lifetime.

Kinsale had rarely seen two visitors so hungry for and appreciative of its finest and biggest lobsters, and of the Muscadet they ordered to wash the shellfish down.

With no instructions about how to spend their day, and being unused to spending their time sight-seeing, they sat prodding lobster shells in the tiny quay side restaurants and debating how to occupy their time in the morning.

'We could hire a boat and go sea fishing.'

'But we'd be out of touch if the office rings,' said Kerrigan.

'Sure, we'll be out of touch, whatever we do. But we could get the skipper to put in to a quay long enough to make a check-call to the hotel and to McKeown around lunchtime, before he takes off for the Glue Pot. We could get some sandwiches made up, and take some bottles.'

'OK. Let's see what the weather's like, but if it's fine enough, we'll do it.'

'Excuse me interrupting, gentlemen.' An American, who Kerrigan recognised as one staying at the same hotel, leaned his chair back from a nearby table. 'I don't wish to be rude, but if I heard you correctly, you are planning some sea fishing tomorrow?'

'Probably.'

'That is in fact what my friend and I were planning, so, I thought, if it wouldn't be an intrusion… I would be honoured if you might let us join you. We'd be happy to share the costs, and with four of us we might hire a bigger boat.'

Kerrigan and Connolly looked at each other and shrugged. 'If you like,' said Connolly. 'But we'll book it on our hotel bills, and you give us your half in cash.'

'Fine,' said the American. 'It sure is good to make your acquaintance.' He held out his hand. 'My name's Robert Sanchez. Everyone calls me Bobby. My friend here is Dan.'

*

'Here, Pat,' said the landlord, I just thought I ought to check that those two men yonder had a fresh bar of soap in their bedrooms, so I went upstairs and when I was in the room of one of them I couldn't help noticing that he kept his passport in a drawer of the bedside cabinet. And minding what we were talking about I just let it, like, fall open. It says that that one there, with the stripy tie, is a Government Servant. What do you think of that?'

'Blinking spy, if you ask me,' said Cooney, knowingly. 'Hey, I haven't got any soap in my bedroom.'

'I know, but what do you think?'

'I think that this thinking game is very thirsty work,' said Cooney, nodding at the Bushmills.

'Where are you going to try tomorrow, gentlemen?' Cooney shouted across the room.

'Where do you recommend?'

'Well, there's Mahony's Bay, Victoria Bay, or Lamb Island, Brown Island or Heron Island. Or if you want to walk down by the golf course, there's the Wash. It depends. What are you fishing with?'

'I beg your pardon?'

'Watson's Fancy? Black Jungle Cock? Soldier Palmer? Have you got all these? Shall I show you my fly box? I might have some spares I could set you up with for tomorrow.' Cooney's fly box was in the bedroom passage, with his waders. When he came back into the bar he told the landlord to join him with a map of the Lough and he went to sit with the Englishmen.

'This is most kind of you. Would you like a drink?'

'There's no need for that at all,' said Cooney, adding quickly, 'but if you insist, we are drinking Bushmills, the black label. I reckon that if you gents are going to drink the same it would be cheaper to go for the whole bottle.'

At midnight, with Cooney lending a hand tidying the glasses the landlord said: 'You don't think they're Revenue men, do you, Pat.'

'I don't. In any case, they're English, you said it yourself. And I'd reckon that Revenue men are more used to strong liquor than those two.'

'You're probably right. But what a coincidence, them knowing that English reporter chap who's staying back where you come from.'

'Aye, the world is full of coincidences,' agreed Cooney.

*

Tuesday, June 6, 1967

Eli Bogart started at the German-owned farm that was furthest from Dublin. He reckoned the chances of finding Ritter were about one in ten, and to make that one chance was going to take time. But if Ritter was still in Ireland the best way to find him was to go where he knew the reporter had been.

The farmhouse had once stood proudly in Georgian-English style, but half of the concrete-clad brick facade had been blown away, leaving what used to be a drawing room open to the elements. A stable block had been gutted and a barn burned to the ground. There was ash, cinder and charred wood everywhere.

As he rounded the corner of the house he was confronted by a tall man with cropped iron-grey hair. He held a rifle across his waist with his hand covering the trigger guard.

He snapped at Bogart: 'What are you doing here?' He had a clipped mid-European accent.

'Hello, sir...' said Bogart, 'I wonder if you could help me, I'm looking for a friend.'

'What are you? American?' asked the man, trying to place Bogart's accent.

'Polish.'

'You're an ex-Pole, if I am any judge,' he sneered. 'What are you doing skulking around here?'

'As I said, I'm looking for a friend. I wonder if you might help me, he's—'

'There are no friends of yours around here.' The man gestured with his rifle, swishing it in the direction of the farm gate. 'Now get off my land, and don't come back.'

'He's called Ritter. I wondered—'

'Get off my land.'

Bogart shrugged his shoulders and walked away. He had parked his car, a Vauxhall Viva borrowed from his embassy in London, outside the village store. He walked into the shop.

'Twenty Marlboro, please.'

'Sorry, we don't keep them.'

'Stuyvesant?'

The grocer indicated his stock of cigarettes. 'Would Benson and Hedges be to your liking at all?'

'Thank you.' Bogart put a ten-shilling note on the counter. 'Actually, I wonder if you could help me. I'm trying to find a friend of mine. I know he was near here not long ago, probably up at the farm. But I should think that in a place like this you'd spot strangers easily enough. The guy I'm looking for is taller than me, a bit over six feet, around a hundred and seventy pounds, dark hair, drives a blue Sunbeam...'

The grocer smiled at the amount of detail. 'Sounds more like a wanted poster than a friend. Reporter, is he, your man?'

'That's the one!'

'Well he was in here a couple or more weeks ago, on a Monday or Tuesday morning. He had a Cork Dry Gin and tonic and bought forty – no sixty – Rothmans and he smoked four of them in here. He bought me a drink, too.' The shopkeeper thought for a moment; Mrs Kilbane had come in for some butter while the young man was talking, and she'd said something about making sandwiches from the leftovers of the Sunday joint. 'A Monday,' he said.

'I'm sorry,' said Bogart, recognising the hint; 'I didn't realise you served drink. I'd like one of those dry gins and tonics, plus whatever you'd like to take yourself.'

'That's very pleasant of you, sir,' said the grocer. 'With you I'll just take a cup of tea.' He poured a healthy measure of gin into a glass, flipped the top off a bottle of tonic, placed them on the counter and went into his back room to put the kettle on.

When he returned Bogart asked him: 'Have you any idea where he went when he left here?'

'Not at all. Though I know where he should have gone. Or, to put it another way, I know where I think I would have gone if I'd been him.'

'Where's that?'

'Straight back to Dublin.'

'And what's the quickest way back?'

'I don't doubt that it's most likely the way you came here,' said the grocer. 'But when I said straight back to Dublin I didn't mean the quickest way. The road to Dublin is the road outside here. The fast way is down the hill. Your man went up it.'

'Perhaps he wasn't going to Dublin, then. Perhaps he was going somewhere else?'

'I don't know about that. If you go uphill, you eventually come to Dublin much the same. All roads lead to Dublin, as the saying goes. Or the roads around here do, to say the least. But when that young man was here it was a nice sunny morning, and though we may not have your motorways here we have some roads that are slower than others, and some that are a little prettier and might appeal to a motoring man who's not in such a great hurry.'

Bogart finished his drink. 'I'll go that way, too,' he told the grocer.

'If I were you I'd go the fast road, myself. He's got few weeks' start on you!'

Three miles along the slow road Bogart pulled into a garage and asked for two pounds worth of petrol. It brought the tank to half full, but he was calculating on stopping at every garage along the route. As the attendant took the notes he asked whether he'd seen his friend who he thought was holidaying in the area: a young man with a blue Sunbeam.

At the second garage he asked the same question.

'A blue Sunbeam, you say? Would that be the Rapier or the Alpine now?'

'Rapier.'

'And you're a friend of the driver of it?'

'He's about six foot two.' Recalling the shopkeeper's report, he added: 'He chain-smokes.' The garage attendant appeared about to change his mind.

'No sir. Not around here.' As Bogart drove off, the attendant said to his wife: 'Now there's a funny thing. I would have sworn he was looking for that young Englishman, Mr Ritter, except I know for a fact that he doesn't smoke.'

*

'What you never told me,' said Ritter to Dr Morell, 'is what happened to Eva.'

'What do you mean?'

The two men were sitting at opposite sides of the dining table, at right angles to the window, with teacups and almond cake in front of them.

'You've told me that Hitler escaped from the Bunker, or anyway that you got him out of it. Obviously the will and the marriage certificate were either completely phoney, or postdated. Maybe it was all a red herring to fit in with the story of death in the bunker.'

Morell didn't elucidate, so Ritter continued: 'But whether Adolf married Eva at all, the question is what happened to her. You can't tell me you spirited your Führer away and left his bride in the bunker.'

'Of course they were married. There was a proper ceremony with a notary. There was Champagne and cakes, and rings, like at any other wedding. I was there. There was a proper wedding certificate. I don't understand what you are talking about.'

'Of course you do, Doctor. I'm talking about why you chose this place – because as you've already explained, or at least I interpreted for you, it's the same height as Braunau. 'And I'm talking about who you chose it for. And that's Adolf and Eva. Mr and Mrs Hitler.'

Ritter had woken in the early hours with the realisation that something in the story was missing. He'd felt confident about Cully, no problems there; but something was missing. He went downstairs to Maire's kitchen, made himself a cup of instant coffee and took it back to bed. He tried to review everything that had happened. It was no good, he would have to resort to his notebooks, and there were now so many that it was going to be a laborious process.

Hours later, only about halfway through the pile, he looked at the list of names on the inside of the cover. Five who died and were buried, without family, in the parish churchyard. Father Dennis had joked about why he was surprised that men died in an unmarried state. But Hitler was married! So why had he, smart reporter that he believed he was, been looking for a single man?

The answer – he now had to start again at the beginning with his notebooks – was that, apart from saying that he had met Eva on the occasion that he flew to provide treatment for her boss, Hoffman, and, incidentally, the first day he had met Hitler, Morell's disjointed narrative had never mentioned her.

Hitler had been drugged and carried to a car. The sequence of events, at least those where Morell's account concurred with history's had been, the wedding, the dictation of the will to a secretary, poisoning the dog Blondi – to prove that the cyanide pills would work – and then the suicide performance.

Ritter was frantically transcribing page after page of shorthand. He had already done it several times, he knew the story. But now he was studying the detail.

We carried him up to a car...

So, what, did Eva walk beside him? She must have been present in the bunker because Hitler was planning that they would die together. Could Morell and the generals have rescued their Führer and left his wife there to die, or to be captured? What would their leader have said about that, when the morphine wore off?

No: she must certainly have come out of the bunker with the others. She could have been dropped in Bavaria, en route, but the likelihood was that she would have stayed with her new husband, if she could. Another thing: at the time of the escape the world was unaware that Hitler had married at what he thought was the eleventh hour. Even if anybody was looking for him, they wouldn't be looking for a couple. But in fact nobody had been looking for him; Morell and Bormann had done their job brilliantly, even providing the body – the two bodies – for the Russians to find. And there was another story – whose bodies had actually been used for the cover-up? – but that could wait for another day.

So, if Cully was Hitler – and there could be little doubt about that – where now was Mrs Cully? She had not been buried with her husband... so had she, newly widowed, departed for South America after the funeral? Did the Nazi fugitives also provide escudos or pesetas to fund her escape?

The only other, even remote, possibility was that Ritter should have been looking for a man and wife, rather than for a single man. But that did not bear thinking about. Cully was it, the scars on his back were the clincher. So where was Eva?

The secret, like so many secrets, was still with the fat perspiring doctor.

He lifted the teapot and offered to refill Morell's cup, but the doctor shook his head, so he filled his own. Mrs Morell, ever the anxious hostess, took it from him, saying, 'Here, let me get this topped up for you.'

'It's only fair to tell you,' Ritter stirred his spoon slowly round the cup, 'I know all about Cully.'

'Mr Cully?'

'All right, Mr Cully. You made a couple of mistakes. Only slight ones, given the nature of the entire operation, but they were deadly ones. First, you should never have allowed his body to be laid out, as they call it here, prepared for burial – you should have done that yourself, because the lady who did it, and I have interviewed her, remembers the marks from the assassination attempt, the *Attentat*, where all the splinters hit him. Second, it was a gross idiocy to pay for the funeral with dago currency: you should've exchanged it into Irish punts yourself, first.'

'You are simply talking in riddles to me. I do not understand all this.'

Mrs Morell put a reheated teapot, and a clean cup and saucer in front of him. Pouring it, he told the doctor: 'You can see that I am going to get it. You know that I will fathom it all eventually. Did the Fourth Reich also send funds for Mrs Cully? How did she get out? And, more important, where did she go to?'

There was going to be an earth-shattering follow-up in this. Because after Ritter had amazed the world with the up-rooting of Hitler, and the unearthing of Hitler's presumed-dead doctor, he was going to astound the universe by discovering Hitler's presumed-dead wife! And she might even still be alive!

But Morell told him: 'My friend, I do not know what you are talking about. I know nothing about a Mrs Cully.'

The Führer, he said, had not at first planned for Eva to die with him. He asked Morell to try to persuade her to go to her family in Munich. Later he asked Hoffman, who was probably the last person to leave the city by car, to take her to Bavaria with him. He even asked Hanna Reich to persuade her to let her fly her out of danger. But Eva had refused all the efforts, and it was after that that Hitler asked her to marry him. There had been a simple ceremony, attended by the inner circle of the Bunker staff. At this stage Hitler had written his will but had not yet finally decided on a time for his suicide, which was why he was still taking the glucose shots that Morell had been able to substitute.

'Of course Eva – by the way, she had signed the wedding certificate Eva Hitler – came with us, when we left. They had to stay together until the end, and they did. They are together now, wherever. There is no reason for me to lie to you. There have been enough lies.'

*

'Here's a man,' said Maire quietly, nodding in the direction of a swarthy stranger, 'who's looking for a chap with a Sunbeam Rapier.' Ritter, watching the landlady start pouring his pint, turned to study him. Short, wiry, wearing dark blue trousers and a blue short-sleeved shirt, his hair was short and curled closely to his scalp. Not a fighter, perhaps a planner; not a man to play chess or bridge with, not if you wanted to win.

Ritter feigned deep thought. 'A Sunbeam Rapier? I don't think there is one round these parts.'

The stranger offered him a cigarette.

'Don't use them, thanks.'

But Bogart had registered the nicotine stained fingertips, and the strange lilt in an accent that, while he couldn't place it, was definitely not Irish.

'You know these parts pretty well, then?'

Ritter shrugged.

'Well, there's a Rapier parked outside this very bar,' he said, drawing thoughtfully on his cigarette. 'With English plates.'

'Really?' Ritter went outside to look. The borrowed 1100 had been removed, obviously by its owners, and in its place stood the two-tone blue Rapier. Crossing the road from the doctor's house, Ritter had been too preoccupied with the story to notice it.

Bogart asked Maire whether she had a room for the night. She told him she'd be surprised if there was a room available for bed and breakfast for miles around, not this side of Dublin, it being the middle of summer.

Unperturbed, Bogart ordered a drink and a dish of stew and took them over to the window for his lunch.

*

Partly to keep out of the new stranger's way, and also to avoid Bayer, when he came back from his search for somewhere locally to stay, Ritter had taken his lunch – his usual Guinness and stew – to his room, to eat on his lap. As he finished, there was a tap at the door and he opened it to see Maire standing there. He invited her in.

'Can you and me have a little talk?' she asked. And when Ritter nodded, she sat on the bed beside him.

'Excuse me asking. I know that it's none of my business and any guest at this inn is entitled to total privacy. But what exactly are you doing here? Do you mind me asking? I ask now, because, after that foreign-looking man arrived this afternoon there's a couple more, now, looking for you, this time they're English and, I'd say, official looking. What are you doing? You're not really a reporter from London, are you? Are you on the run? I might as well tell you that I noticed those two Irish boyos who you were talking to last week.'

'A couple more? Two, you mean? English? Oh bloody hell!'

'It's just that, you know, if you are on the run, or something, I thought we... Well, young Deirdre's not the only one round here who's taken a bit of a shine to you, you know... Perhaps we should help you, somehow. At least, if we were sure it was the right thing to do.' She laid a hand on his thigh, and he placed his hand over it.

'Thanks, Maire. That's great. But if you give me a few minutes I'll sort something out and give you a shout. These Englishmen, do they know I'm here?'

'Not absolutely, but they're hanging about.'

'OK. Give me a few minutes to think.' Maire squeezed his leg and he put his arm round her and pecked her cheek, then put his hand under her elbow and lifted her the short distance to the door.

'You're a sweetheart,' he told her as she left the room. 'Just give me a short while to think.'

He thought. Question: What do they know, the English and the presumed Israeli? Answer: They know I'm here, they probably know Morell's here, they probably know as much as I did when I last left London; that is that Hitler didn't die in the bunker. They must think that by now I know where the body is buried.

Question: what will they do next? Answer: What would I do next? I'd do nothing. Wait for the next move.

Question: What do they expect me to do?

Answer: Find the grave.

He went to the door of Maire's private sitting room.

'I'm checking out tomorrow, Maire. I don't mind anybody knowing that. But what I don't want anybody to know is that I'm coming back, almost certainly the day after. So I'll pay to keep the room on – so don't let it. And keep the fact that I'm coming back a secret, will you?'

'Of course I will,' said Maire.

'And don't worry, love. I'm not on the run. Anyway, not in the way you mean.'

Ritter went to the kiosk outside and phoned McKeown on one of the newsroom lines. Picking up a telephone handset was now the only time that he felt the need for a cigarette, and he was content that it wasn't a craving for nicotine that brought that on, merely the fact that for all his working life he had probably never used a telephone without holding a cigarette between his fingers. That was just habit, routine. He expected that he would get the same reaction when he next rolled a piece of copy paper into a typewriter. But it was merely custom, not an insatiable appetite or addiction for narcotics.

'Do you really reckon the news desk phone is tapped, Bill?'

'Pretty sure.'

'I'll ring you on it in a minute, then. I've got most of the story sorted. Only there's a new development coming, and that's better than you could imagine in your wildest dreams. But I've got to lay a bit of a false trail. When I ring back I'll need a ticket to Munich. Have you got anybody standing by to do a baby-sit?'

'There's Dublin? I sent them to Kinsale to lay a false trail. And I've got Merry on standby.'

'I really need a heavy, Bill, to look after Morell while I'm out of town. Can we make it Merry?'

'If you ring now, you'll get him in the Glue Pot. Ring him, then ring me on my own line in a couple of minutes. But first, tell me what about the new development?'

'I'd forgotten – we'd forgotten – or at least overlooked, the missing link.'

'What's that?'

'Eva.'

'Kinnell!'

'I knew you'd say that!'

When he rang the newsdesk's tapped phone, Ritter said: 'I've found what we were looking for. Can you get Monica to fix me a flight to Munich, an hotel there – Four Seasons, by choice – and two hundred quid in travellers cheques, Sterling, not Deutschmarks, I think, to collect at LAP. I'll ring you from there.'

McKeown turned to his secretary: 'Get Ritter a return ticket, open for any flight, Dublin to Munich via London Airport, to collect at Dublin Airport first thing tomorrow, two hundred in Sterling to pick up at LAP, and book him into the Vier Jahreszeiten.'

'There's no need to shout,' she told him.

'P'raps not, sorry.'

'Ritter's off to Munich in the morning,' he told Morris.'

'Ritter's off to Munich in the morning,' Morris told his friend.

'Ritter's off to Munich in the morning,' McKeown told Ted.

*

'It isn't your day,' said Maire when Ritter returned to the Badgers. 'The Irishman's here, now.'

The reporter and the IRA man shook hands and took a couple of pints of Guinness to the corner table.

'You got your car back safely?'

'Yeah, thanks a million for that.' But the sarcasm was lost in the froth of Guinness.

'We've got a problem, Mr Ritter. Or, more accurately, you've got a problem. It's getting like the United Nations over here, and they're all seeking you. The latest lot is, would you believe, the Russians, and – while as you'll understand we want no truck with Communists – I believe I can confide in you sufficiently to say that these people are prepared to deal. In other words, we've got something they want:

information; and they can offer us, well they can give us, certain different types of support.'

He laid his hand flat on the table. 'So, because we've been straight with each other up to now, I'm giving you twenty-four hours' notice that I'm going to tell the Reds where you are. Not, mark you, what you're doing. They seem to know more than I do about that, already. And what I know is precious little, in fact, bugger all.'

He drained his glass. 'Another of the same?' Ritter nodded and waved his empty glass in the direction of the bar to signal refills.

'There's a better idea,' Ritter said. 'Better, at least, than bringing more strangers into this village. And it's genuine information you can give them, too. You can tell them tonight – tell them right now... trade to them – that, first thing in the morning, I'm going to Munich. See what you can get out of them in return for that.'

One outstanding problem was Bayer. He decided to deal him more information – information probably known to most of the people who were looking for him, but a fact so far unknown to the German reporter, and one he knew he would be unable to resist.

'The fact is that, just as Morell didn't die in Berlin, nor did your Adolf.'

Bayer gazed at him, open mouthed.

'When you did your checking-back on Morell and eventually came up with *die Spinne*, you missed the guy he travelled out of Berlin with.'

Bayer gulped. 'Where did he actually die, then?'

'We know they got him as far as Munich. They didn't want the Russians to get their hands on his body. My guess is the family grave.'

'In Braunau?'

'It's worth checking. Trouble is, Morell won't be specific. I'm flying out tomorrow. You can come if you want. I can fill you in on some details on the plane.'

*

Wednesday, June 7, 1967

Ritter had breakfasted with Maire as had become his habit. And now Bayer joined them. It was the full works, usual in an Irish lodging, of fried bacon, two eggs, soda bread, black pudding, pork sausage, and kidneys. A good way to start a new day. And before they had finished there was a banging on the pub door and when Maire opened it Ritter heard a familiar cockney voice greet her with: 'Top o' the milk to you, milady. My name is Merry. I believe I am expected.'

The two *Post* men – who would have acknowledged each other with a mere nod of the head if they met in the Glue Pot – now embraced like long lost brothers. Maire gaped at the picture they presented: Ritter tall and thin and fair-haired, Merry not much shorter but chunky, definitely thick-set with hair like a gipsy and a face like a cross between Henry Cooper and either of the Kray twins; not a man, she thought, who would start a fight in a bar – but a man who could probably stop one, with just a look.

'Is there any more of that going, darling?' Merry gestured towards Ritter's plate. 'I'd give anything I owned for a good Oirish breakfast. Anything!'

Ritter grimed. 'Come in the Lotus?'

'Well, I wouldn't give the Lotus, but I'd give my life. Or my wife's life, if I had one.' He winked at Maire, who had already decided that she would attend to his every need.

As they ate, Merry told how he had caught the ferry and driven through the night to get there. Then Ritter explained about the need to keep prying eyes off the Morells, to let nobody into the house, and generally to baby-sit while he himself was out of town for a couple of days. He had told him, on the phone to the Glue Pot, that the job was about Hitler's doctor.

'I think this pub window could be as good an observation post as any,' he said, licking his lips.

'Just so long as you can get your lovely body between Morell's door and any visitors who might come calling.' He took Merry across the road to introduce him to the Morells as someone who would take good care of them, and returned him to the Badgers just as Maire was putting his breakfast on the table.

No car other than the red Audi had followed the Rapier from the village to the airport, he was sure of that. But when he went to the check-in desk he spotted Irish, English and Israeli faces loitering in the departure hall.

He declined the offer of an in-flight breakfast, but as the aircraft approached the home counties opted for a miniature of Bushmills.

*

With a morning's catch of fifty-four mackerel, the Sally put into Kinsale so that Kerrigan could make a check-call to London. Five minutes later the fishing-boat skipper saw him walking jauntily back along the quay and he started his engines. As Kerrigan leaped aboard he pulled away to resume fishing.

'Make the most of it, my boy,' he told Connolly; 'When we get back to port the good life is over.'

'What's the problem?'

'Apparently the baby we're meant to be sitting has upped anchor and shot off to Munich.'

'What's that?' asked Sanchez.

'Nothing really,' said Kerrigan. 'We were waiting here for a colleague, but he's gone to Munich instead of coming here.'

'Sanchez turned to the skipper of the fishing smack. 'Quick, I've forgotten something. I've got to get back to the dock.'

'But look at the fishfinder, we're right above shoals of mackerel.'

'You can come back to them. You've got to get me back to land!'

'Sure, it's you chaps doing the chartering. You're paying for the diesel. I'll take you wherever you want.'

'It's Dan... The bird has flown. Apparently he's gone to Munich,' the CIA's Dublin staffman yelled down the mouthpiece of the first available telephone.

'Jeeze, it's a good job we don't have to rely on our men on the spot. Don't worry; we already knew he was going there. What we want you to do is you and Sanchez rebase yourselves in a little village where your bird was actually nesting. If you've got a map I can tell you how to get there.'

*

What was disconcerting about the BA Trident flight to Munich was that there was no familiar face on the aircraft. The Englishmen had presumably handed over to a colleague; the Israeli figure at the airport had followed him only as far as the rope barrier of international departures. Then there was almost certainly a Russian, somewhere. Alternatively, the people who were following him might be simply waiting for his arrival at Munich.

Ritter had told Bayer on the flight to London about the people who had been following him.

On the Munich flight he said: 'I'm sorry I was holding out on you about Adolf.'

'All's fair in love and war, I suppose. I should tell you, I have been holding out on you.'

'You mean you knew about it?'

'No: about Morell, I was holding out. I have found his medical diary.'

'His what?'

It's actually a file of his daily appointments with the guy he calls Patient A, dating from about July of forty-two to the end.'

'Shi-i-it, Hermann! That's fantastic.'

He opened the briefcase he was carrying on his lap. 'I'll show you.'

Bayer produced a photocopy of a diary entry showing what were clearly the last days in the bunker. 'Read it.'

For Wednesday, April 18, 1945, there were references to injections administered to Hitler, then:

Tremor of left hand somewhat better, but sleepy. Sleeping at night, but only possible right now with Tempidorms. Since Sunday there has been a large Russian attack at Kustrin and Frankfurt a.d. Oder.

There were morning, afternoon and evening entries for the next few days and then a heading, underlined:

Dismissal

Afternoon, about two o'clock, a Kondor machine starts for Munich. Flew very low across the Russian lines (Juterbork?). Many burning villages. Later crossed the American front. Over Partenkirchen and Bavaria many search lights and ack-ack activity. After some search landed at airport. Neubiberg?

Ritter nodded at the shiny copier paper. 'Can I keep this?'

Bayer nodded.

'This is how you knew Morell hadn't died in Berlin. That clears up one mystery. Is there much more of it?'

'About one hundred pages.'

'Where did you find it?'

'It was stashed at his place at Bad Reichenhall. The Americans looted most of his belongings but they didn't find his notes. Or perhaps they were not interested in them.'

'Are you going to let me read the rest?'

'Sure. When you've filled me in on the Morell and Hitler notes like you promised.'

Going through passport control, changing some currency and joining a short queue for a taxi, there was nobody who appeared to show the slightest interest in Ritter. He was beginning to wish he had not started his silly game. Bayer was following him at a discreet distance, as they had agreed. Suppose nobody else had taken the bait. He had left Morell uncertain and afraid in Ireland. But he had left them with Tom Merry: he couldn't possibly do better than that. He looked over his shoulder as the black Mercedes taxi pulled away from the rank. This had to be the point of contact: nobody could know whether he would go to book in to an hotel, or whether he would drive straight to where he would pretend the graves would be.

It was impossible to tell. Ritter thought a beige Mercedes was tailing his taxi, and then he thought a red BMW was travelling unnecessarily slowly. He grew suspicious of a blue Opel, but none of them turned into the entrance of the Vier Jahreszeiten hotel where he spent a long time talking to the taxi driver about Bavarian beer, while pretending to fumble for his change.

He checked in, put his overnight bag on the double bed in his room, and returned downstairs to enter the bar.

After studying the beer list he raised his eyebrows to summon the barman.

'Let me buy that, Mr Ritter,' said an English voice at his elbow.

'It's all right, thank you. I have plenty of money.'

'Consider it done,' said the stranger. 'Think nothing of it. Be my guest.'

Bill Bond hated his name. To work in intelligence with that surname was near impossible, even in a profession where people regularly used aliases. Colleagues in the office would introduce him with a pseudo Glaswegian accent 'his name is

Bond' – pause for dramatic effect, – 'Bill... Bond.' What made things even worse was that Bill Bond was distantly related to the 'real' James Bond, the ornithologist author, a favourite of Ian Fleming, and from whom the thriller-writer had taken the name of his hero. If anything, it had been tougher on his previous posting, to Madrid, where he had been known as 'Bail Bond', after the insurance motorists were required to take out in case of traffic accidents. Foxcroft's predecessor had posted Bond to Spain only because he spoke fluent German, and he believed that anyone achieving perfect mastery of a language was already too involved in that country to be safely posted there. Going native, they called it. Some colleagues had announced they were considering learning Icelandic to ensure never being posted to Reykjavik. It was Foxcroft who had readjusted the balance, and introduced common sense.

Earlier in the day Bond had had a problem more pressing than his name. As the 'Six' man in Munich he had been told to follow a British reporter everywhere he went. The reporter would apparently lead him to Hitler's true grave. But manpower couldn't arrange the eighteen strong team normally required for twenty-four-hour surveillance, so direct contact could be permitted.

It was vital that London knew the whereabouts of the grave without delay. The competition was already on the job and Bond had to beat it. It was likely that the reporter had contacts in Bavaria: if necessary Bond should tap his phone and bug his room.

Munich Office did not, however, run to tapping and bugging equipment. Could London send some out in a diplomatic bag? – No: he should buy some, it was for sale on every high street in Britain and everyone knew that Germany was at the forefront of such technology. In case of difficulty, he could borrow some equipment from the German police: the job was sufficiently important for Bond to blow his cover.

So Bond had gone to the head of Munich's anti-terrorist squad and, using a card identifying him as a chief superintendent from Scotland Yard, had made his request. The chief of detectives had appeared outraged.

'Tap a telephone! Bug a room! My dear sir! That sort of thing went out with the Gestapo! We do no believe in such methods in the modern Germany! We certainly have no such equipment.' The policeman pressed a button on his telephone console and summoned his deputy.

This man explained that there was actually a statute, dating back to the creation of the Federal German Republic in 1949, which allowed the police, with a court order, to bug and tap both criminal and victim in the case of serious crime. But... he confirmed his chief's assertion that no such court order had ever been issued. To use one would have meant, ultimately, to declare its use, and a liberal German press acted as a fierce watchdog on the freedom and privacy of the individual: anything that looked like interfering with that privacy and which, moreover, smacked of the Third Reich, would be jumped on.

Bond decided to put all his cards on the table and told the policemen about Hitler's grave. London, after all, had insisted that the success of the mission was paramount.

The detectives stared at each other in astonishment. 'But this isn't criminal,' said the chief. 'It's political. Excuse us for a moment.' He and his deputy stepped into the corridor to talk privately. They were soon back.

'If we can share this with you, we will co-operate.'

Bond agreed to that. 'But I thought you had no equipment,' he said.

'We have none, but we know where to get it. Do you have a number in Munich where we can get back to you?'

At three o'clock Bond's phone had rung.

'It was easier than we thought. We decided to borrow the devices from some friends in the CIA. We were really in luck: they already have the room bugged and the line tapped.'

*

Ritter looked at the man beside him at the bar. He was wearing a dark blue suit with wide curving lapels and side vents. The trousers were slightly flared, the shirt blue and high collared, the tie wide with a large knot.

'Who do you work for?'

'Shall we simply say for the home team...Whitehall?'

'How do I know that?'

'Well, we don't actually carry identity cards, old boy.'

'I thought James Bond worked for Universal Export?'

'What are you talking about?'

'I'm talking about your showing me a business card with a phone number on it.'

'Are you serious?'

'Either that, or you can piss off.'

The man produced a card from a pocket on the lower left inside of his jacket, glanced briefly at it, and handed it to Ritter who laughed involuntarily. 'Global Business? You've not travelled far from Universal Export, have you? What's Global Business, when it's at home?'

'It's a weekly business magazine.'

'Why haven't I read it then?'

'It hasn't started publication yet.' Ritter asked the barman for a telephone, and then told the hotel operator his room number and asked for a line. When he dialled the number on the business card, a voice said: 'Global Business.'

'I'm sitting in a bar in Germany with a ponce wearing a Pierre Cardin suit who works for you. Who am I, who is he, and where are we?'

There was a pause. 'I'm sorry, who is calling?'

'That's what I want you to tell me.'

'One moment, please.' Another pause. 'Can you tell me the name of your superior?'

'I have lots of bosses. Try McKeown.'

'Then your name is Ritter. You are probably in the Vier Jahreszeiten in Munich with our representative whose name is on the business card he will show you. If you would like further proof, Mr Porter came round on Monday to this office... And your passport expires in November next year and it was issued by the Liverpool passport office. When you next speak to Mr McKeown, please tell him that Ted Foxcroft sends his regards.'

'Well done,' said Ritter. 'Now, while I'm on, are you this guy's boss?'

'I'm a senior colleague.'

'Well, I'm a senior journalist. And one thing you lot should know is that life is difficult enough for reporters all round the world where tin-pot bureaucrats think all journalists are spies, without your idiots – who actually are spies – passing themselves off as newspaper or magazine employees. You should stop it. And when I get back I'm gonna get one of my bosses to sort it out with one of yours. It's a bloody disgrace.'

'OK, Mr Ritter, point taken. I confess I hadn't thought of that.'

'I like the GB logo, though,' said Ritter, with a smile, and hung up.

He turned to the man in the Cardin suit. 'Right. What do you want to do?'

'I'm at your service. I have a car. I can take you anywhere you want to go. Where is it you want to go, precisely?'

'To the bog, first. Will you order more beer in, while I'm getting rid of the last lot?' Crossing the foyer towards the gents' toilet, Ritter asked the porter, almost under his breath, to book him a rail ticket to Salzburg, urgently, and deliver it to his room. He turned as he opened the toilet door and found the British agent watching him, from the entrance of the bar.

'That's better,' he said when he remounted his bar stool. 'He took a deep draught of the cold beer. What sort of wheels do you have?'

'BMW, two litre, red.'

'Did you follow me from the airport?'

'That wasn't necessary; I was waiting here.'

So, the news desk phone was bugged. 'Is anybody else following me?'

'There's one way to find out. Shall we go for a drive?'

Ritter nodded.

'My name is Bill, by the way. Do you mind if I call you Charles?'

'If you won't mind my calling you 007.'

The man was a fast and competent driver, far more used than Ritter to checking his rear view mirror for tailing cars. He slowed down when the traffic lights were green, and speeded up when they were changing to red, obviously in an effort to ensure that he was always the last car to cross an intersection.

He went through the busiest part of town twice and then sped towards the outskirts. The road sign said Dachau.

'The big Merc – I'll tell you when you can look round – is our transatlantic cousins, and the white Ford is either German or Jewish. They are all locally based. What did you do – put a notice in *Die Welt*? You can look now.'

Ritter peered behind him and watched a black Mercedes followed by a white Taunus race round the corner after them.

'OK,' he said. 'Let's see you lose them.'

'No problem.' The driver slowed behind a big Volvo tractor-trailer with Danish plates. Ritter watched the tailing cars also slow down to maintain their distance. As the motorcade approached a roundabout the BMW suddenly accelerated and, with barely millimetres to spare, squeezed between the truck and the roundabout.

The Volvo's double klaxons blasted like a ship's horn as the driver slewed the articulated vehicle across the road. The BMW raced back in the direction it had come, turned a series of skidding rights and headed back into the centre of town.

'Where to now?'

'Nice one. Back to the hotel.'

'Hang on. If we do that, we've lost them for nothing.'

'Don't be such a pessimist. Consider that was just keeping your hand in.'

Back at the forecourt of the Vier Jahreszeiten Ritter told Bill Bond to keep the engine running, while he collected his shoulder bag.

Bond said: 'By the way, while you're in your room, I shouldn't use the phone.'

'Why not?'

'Oh, you know, just to be on the safe side.'

'Have you tapped it?'

'I give you my word that I haven't. Her Majesty's Government would never countenance such a thing.'

'There should be no problem, then.'

'Someone else might have tapped it.'

'Who, for instance?'

'Anybody. A lot of people seemed to know you were coming.'

'Then I won't use the phone.'

The tickets and a timetable were awaiting collection on the dressing table in his room. He flipped through the pages and found the Munich to Vienna route, checked his watch and took the lift back down to the entrance.

There was no sign of either of the cars that had been following them earlier.

But neither of them noticed a BMW motorbike that, for most of the time, had been ahead of them.

'Head back to the centre and drive around a bit,' directed Ritter.

'We'll only pick up those shadows again.'

'No you won't. The rush hour's starting now. Even if they see us, they'll never get behind us. The traffic's building up.'

'Where are we going?'

'Head in the general direction of the Bahnhof... I'll show you.'

Traffic was building up as the Bavarian commuters headed home. The city's leafy neoclassical squares were blocked with expensive executive transport. The BMW could only crawl along through the old streets.

Outside the station, the car at a standstill, Ritter turned to the driver, said 'Back in a minute,' then opened the door and stepped out. Leaving the door open, he weaved through the traffic, into the portico, caught a quick look at the departures board, flashed his ticket at the disinterested ticket inspector and raced along the platform to board the Vienna train. Karl Bayer, who had been waiting at the station for him, followed him on board.

The man in the Pierre Cardin suit was unable to park his car and follow him into the station.

The rider of the BMW motorbike had less difficulty. He was fast enough to watch Ritter clamber on board the express train as it chugged out on its journey south. He remounted his machine and set off in hot pursuit towards the Austrian border.

Bayer started scribbling in his notebook as the train moved from Germany across the frontier into Austria.

'What are you writing?'

Bayer looked cautiously around, to ensure that nobody in the coach could hear him. 'Following in the Führer's footsteps,' he said. 'In 1938, he flew to Munich, and then went on to Braunau and Linz. He actually did it by car, but otherwise, we are retracing history. I suppose it was the beginning of the war, the annexing of Austria.'

'Beginning of the war? Not much of a battle, was it? The Austrians cheered him all the way.'

'That's not the point. It was the start of the take-over of territories, the land-grabbing that led to Poland.'

'So, what are you writing about?' Bayer pointed to the mountains, some still snow-capped, the Hansel and Gretl houses, the fir trees. 'I'm describing the view for my colour piece.'

They changed trains at Salzburg, and at Linz hired a car, a Volkswagen beetle, and drove to Leonding, Linz and to the town cemetery at Stadtfriedhof. The Hitler family grave, dwarfed by giant fir trees and a yellow-painted church with an onion-shaped spire, was easy to find. An inscription in gold lettering on a black oval plaque explained that, resting in God, were Royal and Imperial Senior Customs Official Alois Hitler, a Pensioned Houseowner. And his Wife Klara.

'That yellow house, same colour as the church, across the road was the family home,' said Bayer. 'There's a children's playground right beside it.'

'How refreshingly Germanic.'

Ritter studied the headstone, which was surmounted by a cross. In the top centre of the cairn-like stone plinth was a photograph of Alois Hitler, a thickly-built man in a bow tie with sparse hair covering his round skull, and a heavy black moustache.

'It's a pity there's no picture of his mother,' said Bayer. 'Hitler really loved her, you know. He said he honoured his father, but he loved his mother. He carried her photograph with him everywhere he ever went.'

Ritter pointed: 'It's there look, very small and round, right at the bottom, hidden behind the flowers. Let's have a drink.'

As they entered the Gasthaus Wiesinger, Bayer told him: 'This is the tavern where Alois died. He had a heart attack going up the steps.'

'Only a Kraut would fall over on his way in to a pub,' said Ritter. 'I wonder whether his son ever read the inscription over the door.'

Hewn in the rough wood lintel was an Austro-Hungarian welcome, which Ritter translated and made to rhyme in English:

Whether Christian, pagan. Jew.
Come in, we've a drink for you.

'They probably wouldn't have thought anything of it,' said Bayer. 'Their family doctor was Jewish.'

'I didn't know that!'

'Doctor Bloch... Hitler also had a Jewish cook, you know.'

'Not for long.'

'Nevertheless.... No, it was Catholics that old Alois didn't like.'

'But Adolf was a Catholic. He was an altar boy,' said Ritter.

'That was his mother's influence. Alois didn't like it. Klara had been Alois' maid – did you know? – before he put her in the family way.' Bayer ordered two beers.

'Alois would have ordered Cognac... Now we're here, what are we supposed to be doing?'

'I don't know, really. I basically wanted to get a look at the place.'

'If Hitler is truly buried with his mother, the body will have to be exhumed.'

'It's only a matter of getting Morell to admit it, Karl. Now I've seen the grave I'll have more chance of knowing whether Morell is telling the truth.'

'It's interesting to think that when Hitler came here, the war had not yet even started, but he had only seven years to live.'

'Yes. Fascinating, isn't it?'

They returned to the VW and drove towards Innsbruck then headed out along the Inn valley to Brixlegge. Although Ritter was satisfied that nobody was following them, he had decided it would do no harm to disappear from the scene for a night. What was important was that people from several countries believed – knew – that he was in the Munich area.

From Brixlegge they took the twenty-minute winding drive to Alpbach, where the colour of the roofs changed from terracotta to chocolate, and every windowsill boasted a window box packed with red geraniums. They booked into the Boglerhof hotel and studied the menu preparatory to what they had planned as a quiet and peaceful dinner.

'My dear Charles!' boomed a friendly Austrian voice. 'How nice to see you again!' Ritter had never stayed at the Boglerhof: he'd never stayed in Alpbach with the benefit of a newspaper's picking up the bill. But he'd spent many boozy nights there after driving down from camp in Germany for weekends acting as interpreter for the Army Ski Association, which was headquartered in this tiny Tyrolean village – the most beautiful in Austria, some said. And the man so pleased to see him was Franz Moser, one of more than three hundred villagers to share the surname, and one of several instructors who had tried without notable success to teach Ritter to remain upright at speed with planks strapped to his feet.

'When you come in winter I am unable to teach you to ski, because you cannot bend the knees, and now you come in summer and I am again unable to teach you because there is no snow!' It was what passed for humour in the remote Alpbach valley.

'*Gruss Gott*, you old bastard! So much for the quiet dinner we were planning,' said Ritter to Bayer. He signalled a waiter. 'Better make that three *Kaiserbiers. Grossen.*'

Forty years earlier there had been no road into the village, which had developed in the twelfth century as a silver-mining town. This accounted for a single traditional architectural style in Alpbach – local builders had seen only one style of house design, and they stuck to it – and a unique dialect. Thursday was *Donnerstag* in Germany and Austria, but *Finsdag* in Alpbach; in Alpbach, spring was *Langs*, instead of *Fruhling*, and girl was *Diandl*, rather than *Madchen*.

Ritter had mastered most of the words and pronunciation and delighted in refreshing his memory over beer and schnapps with his old friend, to the bemusement of his companion, Bayer.

'The tourist season is upon us,' said Franz. 'Yet today we have only three visitors: the two of you and a motorbike man.'

'A motorbike man?'

'Maria said he followed you up from Brixlegge. She was shopping and recognised you in the car and said this man followed your car up here to Alpbach, as though he did not know the way. He's checked in at the Jakober.' Maria, another member of the vast Moser clan, ran a coach and taxi firm that sometimes brought soldiers up from the station.

'Do me a favour will you, Franz? Ring the Jak and ask Schwarzenauer who the guy is, and how long he's checked in for.'

When he came back from the phone in reception Franz said: 'There's a thing! He's German. But from the East. He's just sitting outside on the balcony, staring up this way.'

'What are you doing in the morning, Franz?'

'Nothing special.'

'Have you still got that old Norton?'

'Sure thing.'

'Let's go for a ride on it, after breakfast.'

'Sure. But first, let's have some more schnapps and beer tonight!'

*

As the sun set behind the hill facing the Badgers, a grey Triumph 2000 pulled into the main street and stopped.

Two Americans, Bobby Sanchez and the CIA's Dublin staffman, went into the pub for a drink. Half an hour later they crossed the road and rapped on the door knocker.

'Can I help you?' Merry had followed them out of the pub and, as instructed, interposed his body between the visitors and the door.

'Who are you?'

'Friend of the family.'

The Dublin staffman raised his hat. At that moment, although she and her husband had agreed that they wouldn't do it, Mrs Morell went to the door. It was just a natural reaction. As she prepared to open it she heard an American-sounding voice tell Merry: 'Then, I'm sorry to trouble you but – I wonder – do you know whether Dr Morell is at home? My name's Cohen.'

*

Thursday, June 8, 1967

The Wiedersberger Horn starts its seven thousand feet climb exactly a mile from the village. Franz Moser arrived at the front of the Boglerhof and stood astride his motorbike, revving it sufficiently long and loud to attract the attention of both Ritter and the BMW rider a hundred yards away at the Jakober inn.

Ritter, clutching his shoulder bag, mounted the Norton behind the Austrian and set off so quickly they kicked gravel across the road. They headed east towards the mountain farms, which still functioned as they had for centuries. They passed the Dorfer farmhouses and then, keeping right at all the forks, passed a farmhouse called Rossmoos which, during the ski season, doubled as a mountain inn. Opposite Wurmhof farm they turned down the hill and followed mittlerer Hoehenweg towards the village. Now they were off the roads and speeding over grass, still wet with dew. The BMW followed, but its road tyres found the going less easy than the studded cross-country treads on the Norton. Moser sped along the south bank of the Alpbacher river then skidded left and started up the hill towards the mountain.

Half way up the slope was a bar and restaurant for skiers in winter and for ramblers in summer. Ritter dismounted there, and started to climb the hill.

Moments later the BMW rider propped his machine against the wall of the restaurant, and he too started to climb. Moser watched until the German was out of sight. Then he took a motorcycle tool kit from his pannier.

Five minutes later he raced his Norton up the hill, passing the German, and collected Ritter. The two sped back to the foot of the Wiedersberger Horn and along the Inn valley towards Innsbruck.

When the German motorcyclist arrived breathless at the place he'd parked his bike he found that it was missing a front wheel. Moser had simply unfastened it and rolled it down the mountain.

He and Ritter celebrated their success with a beer and schnapps at Innsbruck airport. Raising his half litre of Kaiser, Moser said: 'Just a minute! What about your German reporter friend? I have just realised – we have left him in Alpbach!'

Ritter took a long draught of the beer.

'Fuck him!' he said.

He had bought a ticket for an Austrian Airlines flight to Vienna, where he connected with flights to Amsterdam, then Newcastle and on to Belfast, where he raced to catch the last Dublin train, took a taxi to the airport, collected his car, and drove swiftly through the night to the village that now felt like a second home, and where he found Merry sitting in his yellow Lotus and listening to BBC World Service outside the door of the Morell's house.

'How's it been?'

'Quiet as the proverbial, since you left. Some Yanks arrived just after you went, but everybody's disappeared now. By the way, that Sunbeam stands out like a pork chop at a Jewish wedding...'

'Like a coloured dog, you mean.'

'No: it stands out like a bulldog's bollocks, since you ask. I've had a word with Maire, and you're to put it in her yard at the back of the pub. It isn't you that people have been looking for, it's your fucking car that gives you away, you prat!'

Slightly stung by the rebuke from his pal, Ritter countered: 'Oh, it's not prominent, like, say, a primrose-yellow Lotus, then?'

'Nobody, Mr Clever-Knickers, is looking for Thomas "The Tank Engine" Merry, esquire; whereas the world and his wife is looking for you, and what they know about you is that you are a long streak of trans-Pennine piss with a blue Rapier. Did you bring me any duty frees, old cock?'

Ritter parked the Rapier in the backyard of the Badgers, handed Merry a carrier bag containing a bottle of Scotch and 200 Camels – the only brand of cigarette they had left on the Austrian Airlines flight, and told him: 'Go and have a kip. Use my bed. I'll sit here for the rest of the night. See you at breakfast. And don't smoke in my bedroom, if you don't mind!'

ELEVEN

Friday, June 9, 1967

Breakfast – now it was Merry, Maire and Ritter eating together – was interrupted by a phone call.

'No,' they heard the landlady say; 'Mr Ritter was here, but he left a couple of days ago, day before yesterday, I think… I think he said he was going to Germany – well, either Germany or Austria – I'm not sure, now… Oh, yes, I thought I recognised the voice… well, if Mr Ritter rings here, I'll tell him you were asking for him… You're where? Linz? How do you spell that? Right-oh. Not at all, bye-bye.'

Rejoining the reporters, she told them, 'That was your German friend – the one who held the Guinness up to the light – he says if you call here I am to tell you that he has somehow lost you and is waiting for you at the Post Hotel; in Linz.'

A day occupied by almost non-stop travel had given Ritter plenty of time to think.

Hitler, he knew, was Cully. The lady who had once briefly styled herself as Mrs Hitler had fled the scene. The common denominator was of course Dr Morell; he had brought his beloved Führer to Ireland, he had whipped up the foreign funds to pay for the burial – of course, he would not have been able to pay for it himself: he could not have even tried to gain access to the possessions he would have been forced to leave in Germany, nor even to whatever fortune he had amassed in his personal bank accounts, because he was believed to be dead. Even losing a fortune and a few paintings would, surely, be a small price to pay for being allowed to continue living. So Morell would have raised the funds to ship Mrs Hitler out of the way. He would know where she had gone, maybe possibly even was still in touch, although that was a remote possibility, he realised.

The previous day, flying from Newcastle to Belfast along Hadrian's Wall, and looking down briefly on his own house, he had fantasised momentarily that Mrs Morell might even be Eva. Well, it was a possibility, another remote one. But, while both he and Bayer had established that there were no extant photographs of the Morells, so he had no idea what Hanni Morell was meant to look like, there were pictures aplenty of Eva – she had, after all, been a photographer's assistant – and the body shape was all wrong. You could do all sorts of things these days with plastic surgery, but you couldn't turn a shortish heavy-boned woman into a tallish slim one.

So he was going to have to confront Morell again, and tell him: 'I know all about Eva.' And see where he went from there.

But there was no rush for that. He would wait for the Morells to get themselves up and about and organised before crossing the road for the daily chat. The Cully grave was, after all, the priority.

He sat in the sunshine on the bench beside the bus stop and watched Merry flick a cigarette expertly so that it bounced on the kerbstone and ricocheted into the drain in the gutter. 'I know now why they call them Camels.'

'You should stop smoking. You'll feel tons better.'

'I've tried that. You get withdrawal symptoms – headaches, sore throat, and colds – suddenly, you've lost the great advantage of killing all the germs that gather in your mouth by sucking poisonous red-hot smoke down your throat. Nothing can live in my mouth, especially germs, so as Churchill said to that bumptious little twit, Montgomery, I both smoke and drink and I am 200 per cent fit. And another thing, when you stop smoking, you drink twice as much, because suddenly you've got nothing to do with your hands, and they are in the habit of going back and forth to your mouth, so now they start doing that reaction with a pint glass, instead of a healthy fag. Have you noticed that? And the same thing applies to food, you put on weight...' He looked at Ritter. 'Except for people built like you. No, Tex, my son. There is nothing to be gained from it.'

'One thing I found is, when you stop smoking you can shag all night long.'

'I'm not sure I'd want to do that,' said Merry. 'But that reminds me... Do you know that nobody here knows your friend is a doctor?'

'Yes. I was surprised at the start that not even the *Garda* knew. But you can see why Morell wouldn't want to tell anybody.'

'I don't know, he presumably has to make a living, somehow.'

'Well, he could hardly bring his certificates over from Heidelberg, could he? But that's a good thought, Tom. It hadn't occurred to me to ask him what he lives on. I know that there was some funding available from South America, possibly via Spain, when his guv'nor kicked the bucket. I don't see why they should be supporting him, now, 20 years later, but maybe they are. Maybe it's his reward for keeping the body out of other people's hands. I'll ask him. Anyway, how do you know that people don't know he's a doctor: how many people have you asked, for God's sake?'

Merry explained that when Maire had asked about the two men's interest in Mr Morell, he had automatically corrected her by saying 'doctor', and this, to Merry's astonishment, had been an even bigger surprise to the pub landlady.

'But it was when you mentioned shagging, that reminded me,' he said. 'I had a chat with that bird from the grocer's shop, Deirdre. She's got threepenny bits like the headlamps on a vintage Bentley – but I don't have to tell you that, because you are in there, my son. She's definitely taken a shine to our Tex. Have you given her one, yet?'

'Nope. Came pretty close, but not yet.'

'Well, don't disappoint her, otherwise the Tank Engine will feel obliged to step in. Anyway, she wanted to know why you called him doctor. When I said it was because he is, or at least was, one, she likewise said, Oh, no he wasn't, and if he was, why didn't he do something about Mrs Brown's arthritis? It's not as if she's that old, but she suffers. Or what about old Mr Brown's chest, even?'

'Mr Brown? I didn't even know there was a Mr Brown.'

'Well you wouldn't. It takes a professional to uncover these things. Facts, we call them, Mr Ritter. Anyway, the lovely Deirdre says he's never been out of bed. He's bedridden with something wrong with his chest, that's all she knows. How long have you been here, Mr Ritter? How come I know more about the people in this village than you do?'

'Did she say whether she had ever seen him, Mr Brown? Did she say what he looked like?'

'She's never been upstairs in all the time she's worked in the stores. Nobody has, well, nobody except our man Morell. She says he just comes in to talk to them. That's what she means: if he was a doctor he'd do something about it, wouldn't he? All Mr Morell – Doctor, as we call him – does is talk to them. And she also told me about this little game with the clock, how he always comes over and takes the napkin off the clock, that the shopkeeper's just put on. She obviously does this to spite him – and Morell their only friend, too.'

Ritter told Merry he needed to bring him up to date. He told him that, since identifying the grave there had been a development: everybody had overlooked one factor – the whereabouts of Hitler's wife. He didn't call her by her proper name. He told Merry about the foreign currency and explained that, while the grave stood as a great story, it needed putting on the back burner temporarily while he pressed the doctor for more details of her whereabouts.

*

'Where I went wrong, where I have been going wrong all along, is in thinking that if they didn't die in the bunker, they must have died somewhere else. You told me I was wasting my time looking for graves, but I didn't believe you. I apologise for that. You see, I've sorted it out. There's no grave because Hitler's not dead. He's across the road. He's living over a bloody corner shop, calling himself Mr Brown! Until this morning I didn't even know there was a Mr Brown. What is he named after? His bloody shirts…? No, of course not. It's bloody Eva! Bloody Ada, more like.' He spread his hands. 'Now… I'd like you to take me over the road and introduce me to Mr and Mrs Brown. Mrs Brown! What a bloody joke!'

'It was a sort of joke, you know,' said Morell. 'But it was never intended to be a funny one. It was actually the Führer's idea. He thought of it. Of course, nobody in England, and not many people in Germany, knew about Fraulein Braun until some time after the war. Everybody in Ireland – and in England, too, for that matter – everybody pronounced her name like brawn. Brown was a very common name; it was as good as any name to use here.'

Doctor Morell raised his body from the table on his huge forearms and walked determinedly to a writing desk, opened a drawer and reached in to it.

When he turned back he was holding a revolver in his fleshy hand, and pointing it at Ritter.

*

'I saw you walking out with that Englishman, the other night, Deirdre. I hope he behaved himself, did he?'

Deirdre put a large white loaf, a half-pound pat of butter and a packet of digestive biscuits on the counter. She took a pencil from her drawer and totted the price up on a corner of the tissue-paper wrapping she used for unpacked goods.

She asked the filling station attendant's wife: 'Anything else? ...You needn't worry yourself about Mr Ritter; he's a perfect gentleman, he surely is.'

The customer added a quarter pound of boiled ham and six brown eggs to the purchase. 'I thought that since you and he are such good friends, I'd tell you that he has another friend round here.'

'I know, they work together, he has a yellow Lotus.'

'Not this one. This one's very Jewish-looking. He came into the garage the other morning and asked after Mr Ritter; only he mentioned that he chain-smoked, so my Micky thought it wasn't him. But I remembered him saying, the other day when he bought all that awful chewing gum, that he'd just given it up. And this man had driven off before I could tell him.'

'Well where is he now, this friend? Did he say if it was urgent?'

'I don't know. But he said he was a friend of Mr Ritter's, and he clearly knew somehow he was here and he said he was looking for him, so he'll not be too far away.'

'Maybe I'd better tell him, then,' said Deirdre.

*

It was, Ritter considered much later, the shock of the doorknocker that did it. Morell had quite clearly not fired a gun in anger, nor in any other type of emotion, in his life. His clammy hand was shaking and swaying, and the heavy shoulders were pumping out gallons of sweat. Ritter had only one serious thought: I hope he's got the safety on. He had handled a few guns during his national service, his firearms instructor had made sure that they all corrected the shakes by holding a handgun with two hands, and pointing it like pointing a finger.

'Over twenty years I have waited and wondered about this day,' said Morell. 'For twenty years we live in peace with no connection with the rest of the world, and no communication except with each other. And now you, an interfering reporter, come to ruin everything, to kill us. But I will tell you this Mr Reporter, you may have killed us, but before you do that I shall kill your busy-body self!'

Ritter looked at Morell. There was no way, he knew, that the doctor intended to pull the trigger. Another thing the firearms instructor had said was that if someone intends to fire a gun, he fires it: only in the movies do people stand about pointing guns and explaining their motives.

He looked at the blustering doctor who pointed the gun in his general direction, but continued to wave it about as he spoke.

'Now look here, Doctor Morell...'

'Don't speak to me!' His voice crescendoed.

Ritter half rose from his chair. That was a mistake. Then the doorknocker clattered against its brass plate.

Morell made a choking sound and suddenly Ritter saw the end of the barrel erupt. He fell to the ground, clasping his shin, which felt – he had experienced the feeling – as if a freshly shod horse had kicked it. Later, it seemed like entire seconds later, he heard the report of the gun.

Mrs Morell, who had been standing by the door, opened it to find Deirdre standing there.

'Is Mr Ritter here?' she asked, at the precise moment that the gun went off.

Mrs Morell looked over her shoulder and her face paled. 'I'm sorry,' she said. 'He's busy at the moment.' And closed the door quickly.

Deirdre had never heard a revolver shot in her life. If any of the other residents heard anything they might have put it down to a solitary poacher, or even a car backfiring. Merry, who had been in a few trouble spots in his time, thought for a moment that he recognised the sound, and then decided that it was absurd.

*

'You stupid bastard,' said Ritter, rolling around on the floor and trying to staunch the blood oozing from his leg. 'You've shot me!' It was inadequate, but the only thing he could think of to say.

Morell, who had been shaking with rage, was now quivering with fear. His eyes went wide. He dropped the gun and sank to his knees, clutching his heart. He put his forehead on the carpet, and vomited noisily.

'For God's sake,' said Ritter. 'There's got to be some antiseptic and some bandage here, in a doctor's house!'

He turned round to see that Mrs Morell had fainted. He pulled a napkin off the table and tied it around his shin. 'You great fat bastard! You've broken my fucking leg.'

He grabbed another napkin and crawled over to where Morell was lying, mindful of stories about inquests he had covered where people had died by choking on their own vomit. He wiped under the doctor's mouth. Then he sat him up and attended to his own problem.

There was blood everywhere. And Ritter was crying with the shock of the pain. He had a vague idea that he should apply a tourniquet, but as far as he could remember from first aid lessons the pressure point would be behind the knee, not an easy place to apply it, and he thought that blood should be allowed to flow to a break to prevent gangrene.

He rolled back his trouser leg, took of his right shoe and the blood-sodden sock and prodded the grey-faced doctor. 'Come on, you're the quack. Do something about this bloody break.'

Morell recovered enough of his composure to scrabble across the carpet on his knees and attend to his wife. He checked that she had suffered no damage from the fall and was breathing normally. Then he placed a cushion beneath her head, put her head on one side and crawled back to Ritter.

He held the reporter's leg. 'Let me have a look at your leg. Does this hurt?'

'What do you mean, does it hurt! Of course it fucking hurts. You know what it's like if you only bang your shin. What do you think it's like what some fucker shoots it?'

'Can you move your toes?'

'I can't even feel my toes.'

'Try to wriggle them... It's not broken,' said Morell, as Ritter's toes moved. He shoved himself to his feet, panting heavily, then left the room and reappeared, still swaying, with a bottle of liquid and a bandage, and attended to Ritter's wound.

'The blood will stop in a few minutes. But I will have to dress this again, later today. Now, give me a hand with Mrs Morell, will you.' Between them, Ritter moving about on his knees, they manhandled the doctor's wife on to a sofa as she recovered consciousness.

'Oh, Theokins,' she said softly, adding, in German, 'What on earth have you done?'

Ritter hopped into the kitchen and washed the blood from his hands, his foot, and his damaged leg and then rinsed his sock. Morell came in and helped him dry his leg.

'How the hell am I going to get about? What am I going to do now?' he asked.

Morell looked at him unsympathetically. 'Limp,' he said.

*

Merry was standing on the doorstep as Ritter, ashen-faced, emerged.

'What happened in there?'

'The fat fucker's shot me.'

'Jesus! Was this over Eva?'

'More or less. Give me a hand.' The two reporters scuttled across the road, Ritter hanging on to Merry's strong elbow.

'Do we involve the law, now?'

'We can't, can we?'

'Do you want me to ring McKeown? We can't have Fleet Street's finest being shot down by krauts...! Do you want me to take you to a hospital?'

'No need. Morell's treated it. He's a doctor, remember?'

'Ah, yes. But only you and I know that.'

Back in his bedroom at the Badgers, Ritter changed his trousers and again rinsed his socks under the tap. He examined the trousers, there were two bullet holes in the leg; the right sock had one, big, hole. Useful souvenirs, for when he told the story, he reckoned. Perhaps he shouldn't have washed the sock. The bandage was bloody, but not, he thought, likely to seep through the leg of his other trousers. A clean sock, with a handkerchief between it and the bandage, should help. He washed his face and, clinging on to the stair rail, hopped down to the bar.

Maire asked Ritter, quietly: 'What's happened to you?'

'I was a bit stupid, that's all, and I've banged my shin.'

'Oh, I know what that's like. It's really painful. Still, it'll soon stop hurting. But the shin, oh, I think that's the most severe pain you can ever have.'

'Almost,' said Ritter. 'The most severe pain is migraine. The next is maybe childbirth. I suppose a crack on the shin comes somewhere after that.' Ritter, regretting his smart-arsed response to Maire's genuine concern, took a chicken sandwich to his bedroom and then tried, unsuccessfully, to sleep.

At about four o'clock he went back downstairs, his leg aching and stiff. Merry was sitting in his Lotus. He waved and walked painfully across the road and knocked on the Morell's door.

'Ah, Mrs Morell... How are you feeling? Are you better, I hope?'

'Yes, thank you, Mr Ritter... I'm afraid you can't come in.'

'But I have to.'

'Well, you can't. You must understand why. It's better if you don't come back here again. Ever. Just do whatever you think you must.'

'I might do that eventually, Mrs Morell,' said Ritter. 'Meanwhile I've got to see your husband. My leg's still bleeding. I can't drive to a hospital. And I don't want to go to another doctor or phone for an ambulance, not with a bullet wound...'

Ritter sat on a chair with his leg propped on another for Dr Morell to examine it.

'Here's the problem,' the doctor said, peering into the wound with a magnifying glass. 'I told you it wasn't broken. But there's a bit that's broken off.' He took a pair of tweezers from his bag and prodded inside. When he withdrew the instrument it was holding a piece of bone, about the size of a sixpence.

'Now it will stop bleeding,' the doctor said. Next, from his bag, like a conjuror, he produced a small white rubber sphere, which he shook, and then pressed to puff powder like talc into the wound. 'This is a sort of antibiotic Polyfilla, it will form a body for the skin to heal over.'

'Should I get myself a walking stick?'

'It will heal better if you don't. By the way, how do you rate the pain?'

'What do you mean? It's bloody painful, that's how I rate it.'

'As painful as your migrainous neuralgia, would you say?'

'It's difficult to compare. No, I suppose it's not. No, of course it's not.'

'No problem for you, then, is it?'

'Tell you what, doctor; I'm not really sure about this pain. Let's you and I walk over to Mrs Brown's and consider whether I should really buy some Anadin, or perhaps even one of her blackthorn walking sticks.'

'No, Mr Ritter. I don't want to go over there.'

'But I want you to, doctor. My friend and I could just cross the road and barge our way in – my pal is really good at that sort of thing. I don't need you to introduce me to the Browns, but it would be better if you did.' He patted his waistband. 'After all, now, I have the gun.'

'You won't shoot me, I know that. If I take you to see Mr Brown, you can only do that much. Only see him. He is a dying man. You must not speak to him, and you must leave when I tell you to leave.'

It was, thought Ritter, a start. 'I'll agree to that,' he lied.

'And you must leave the gun here.'

'I'll give it to my friend as we cross the road.'

Once inside the Browns' shop Morell told Ritter to wait a few minutes while he went upstairs. Ritter smiled at Deirdre.

'What's the matter with your foot?' she asked. 'You're limping. And you look as white as a sheet.'

'It's my leg, not my foot. I've just barked my shin, that's all.'

'I did that once. I know, it really hurts.'

Morell appeared at the foot of the stairs and beckoned him to follow him up.

'Are you going upstairs?' asked Deirdre. 'I've never been up there.'

'Remember,' whispered Morell. 'You mustn't say anything.' He led him into a bedroom at the head of the stairs. 'Nothing at all.'

*

The curtains were three-quarters drawn against the afternoon sunlight and what brightness invaded the room made little impact on the dark furniture. It was heavy, early Victorian, and the suite, consisting of ceiling-high double wardrobe, dresser with mirror, wash stand with jug and bowl, armchair with hand embroidered antimacassar, and the double bed virtually filled the room.

The bed itself was neatly made up, perhaps by the doctor in the few minutes before Ritter had followed him up, and was massive, dark wood with square corners and head- and foot-boards like dining tables with inlaid gold paint. On the side nearest the window, furthest from the bedroom door, lay a skeletal form, old, almost bald, his skinny arms – protruding from the sleeves of a blue and white striped pyjama jacket on top of the quilted bedcover – merely bones. The skin, stretched taut across the skull, was shiny and translucent. The eyes stared unseeing at the ceiling. The mouth sagged open.

It was impossible for Ritter to avoid the comparison: Adolf Hitler looked like a concentration camp victim.

Morell touched the bony wrist to signal his arrival in the bedroom.

'This,' he whispered in German, 'is the English reporter I told you about.'

The eyes flickered in momentary recognition as the doctor continued: 'He wants to meet you.' Again, the eyes moved, but not far enough to meet Ritter's. The reporter moved around the foot of the bed until he had eyeball contact with the most evil man in the history of the world.

Here he was confronting the man against whom Genghis Khan, Attila the Hun, and Caligula paled into insignificance. Who had, albeit briefly, controlled almost half the world. Who was personally, wholly, exclusively responsible for the Second World War. For the deaths of six million Jews. For maybe twenty million Russian troops and civilians, a quarter of a million British servicemen, and an unknown number, between two and three million, of Germans, of which Captain Karl Ritter, leader of an SS motor cycle platoon, husband of an English wife and father of a son who would not be able to remember his father, had in 1940 been but an insignificant statistic.

'Hello,' said Ritter. He cleared his throat and tried again. 'Hello, Mr Hitler.'

'I told you,' hissed Morell. 'Don't speak.'

'Ask him... You ask him, if he's got anything he wants to say,' whispered Ritter.

The doctor talked almost under his breath to his patient, and the sometime Führer replied in what appeared to be little more than exhalations of breath.

'I've told him that you've promised that if you write about him, you won't give any clue as to where he is,' said Morell. 'He hasn't long for this world, and he's very worried about being found by the Jews.'

'There's one condition to that,' replied Ritter. He was staring at the deathly figure on the bed. He looked like a waxwork. 'You must get out of him his last testament, his message to the world, for me, from his deathbed.' He looked again at the slumped figure. 'And you must do it before he kicks the bucket.'

'That much,' whispered Morell, 'I think I'm sure I can promise you. But, as you can see, not today.' As they went together down the house stairs into the shop they were greeted by Deirdre.

'Did you meet up with your friend, Charles?' she asked. 'The one who came here looking for you? You know, the Jewish-looking one?'

*

Limping, Ritter went straight to the telephone kiosk and rang McKeown on a newsroom phone. He told him to go straight to the phone in the Glue Pot and await a call. But when he dialled it, Ritter found it engaged. He dialled repeatedly until he heard McKeown's familiar voice.

'Bill, I know you'll think I'm buggering you about, but nip round to the Blue Anchor, will you? Believe me, it's worth it.' They had bugged the news desk, they might have bugged the newsroom – and who knows? – even the Glue

Pot. But they couldn't have bugged every phone in every pub in Fleet Street.

Minutes later he was connected to a breathless McKeown.

'We need a snapper, Bill, and we need him now. We have to move very quickly. Plus, we need Hugh Trevor-Roper – can you get him quickly?'

'Kinnell, Chas! You've found the... you've found the lady?'

'Better than that! But we need an expert. More than that, Bill, I can't tell you now. I daren't tell you. But I think really you ought to come over yourself. I need to talk this through with somebody, and there's nobody else at all I can trust.'

'You've got Merry...'

'No, Bill. I might trust him like a brother, but I am not gonna share this one with another reporter.'

'OK. OK. I had nothing planned for the weekend. Kinnell! I can't get Trevor-Roper. We need someone we can control; I'll try to get Stan Blenkinsop, there's no greater military historian, and he owes me. How are we going to find you?'

'Communicate via Monica, on the newsroom phones, or at her home tonight, and I will meet you wherever. Hopefully at Dublin Airport.'

Alone in his bedroom at the Badgers, Ritter sat with his head in his hands. For the second time that day he was in tears: not from pain this time but from self-pity and a sense of stupidity and frustration.

What a prat. What a PRAT! A reporter, a Fleet Street pro, a world traveller, a BTO, a man who recorded history in the making. And when he gets the greatest chance of the world's biggest-ever scoop he says... what does he say? He says: 'Hello, Mr Hitler.'

That's what 'Scoop Ritter' says to the most evil man in the history of the world! *Hello Mr Hitler*!

He'd even played that game at dinner parties where people asked who, if you had the choice of anybody from world history, you would most like to sit beside at dinner.

Most people opted for Jesus; Ritter, awkwardly, usually argued in favour of Doubting Thomas, or even Judas, on the grounds that it might be a better, less biased, account. Somebody usually went for Napoleon and somebody always wanted Hitler.

But nobody ever said: 'And when you sat next to him, what would you say?'

Not *Hello, Mr Hitler*, certainly!

Jesus! His father – the 'war criminal' – had got more out of Hitler than he had. His reward for getting back through shot and shell with the news from Norway that the German Army had had its first meeting with the Allies, the great British army, in a straight fight, and had beaten it hands down, had been a medal – and a quote! Pinning the Iron Cross (first class) on his tunic, the Führer had quipped, 'Next time, Captain Ritter, it must be your own medal, the *Ritterkreuz*! – the Knight's Cross!'

Jesus! No need to tell anybody in the Ritter family that old Adolf had a sense of humour! Except there was to be no next medal. Captain Ritter was to be blown off his motorbike in Dunkirk by a shell from a British warship that did the job so thoroughly nobody ever found the bits. His son had not yet reached his second birthday.

Now, the son sat on his bed and made notes of what he could remember about Hitler's appearance, and listed and described the furniture.

He'd been able to put on a brave and positive front when talking to McKeown, but he knew he had not made a very impressive job of it, so far.

On the other hand, he felt he hadn't done that badly. For a start, he had found Hitler's doctor – that was a cracking good bit of sleuthing, and a great story in its own right – finding a witness to history, a man the whole world, or most of it, believed to be dead. Then he had discovered that Hitler had not – as history showed – died in the Berlin bunker. And if he had been buried somewhere else, Ritter would have found the body. Except, shit, if he had dug up Mr Cully's grave on the grounds that it was Hitler's... Shit! That would not have been very clever – and that was the presumption, only two days ago. That was why Merry had come to help him.

Nevertheless, he had also worked out that Eva hadn't died in the bunker, either. And he had even started the process of tracking her down... That had been good reporting work. Classic, some would say. And then he'd found her. And then he had found *him*! No other reporter, no other reporter in the world, could have done that. Shit! Was that why God and his mother had given him migraine – so that he could stumble onto the scoop of the century? Now he had to calm down, stop blaming himself, even stop congratulating himself. Take it all calmly. Marshal his thoughts. He had, after all, only found Adolf Hitler, alive and well and living over a corner shop! Nothing to get excited about.

*

'I want to talk to the man again tonight,' Ritter told Morell. 'It's important.'

'It's totally out of the question.'

'Yes, but this is vital.'

'No, you'll have to wait until he's able. If he is. Anyway, what's this about your Jewish friend?'

'I promise you, that's not a problem. He's not a friend of mine. He's nothing to do with me. And I've no idea if he's Jewish, and, anyway, he's gone, now... Look, what I was doing the last couple of days was laying a false trail. Lots of people have tumbled to what I am doing. Don't ask me why, it's just impossible to keep secrets these days. But, look... I have kept my part of the bargain. I have kept people away from you. Well, more or less. I am still going to keep my word and stop people getting to you, and, more important, stop them finding out about him. What I want from you in return is a promise that you'll fix me up straight away, like tonight, with his last message to the world. And he's got to give it to me, tonight.'

'Are you saying that when you publish this story you'll say that all this happened somewhere else?'

'I won't necessarily say it, but I'll give that impression.'

'And you won't print anything anyway until Mr Brown has died?'

'Just a minute! You've never suggested that before. But, tell you what, if that's OK with my editor, we'll do it. How long has he got?'

'A day or two, not much longer, I think. But I want one more promise from you,' said Morell. 'Before this story is published – before it is even prepared for publication – I want you to get my wife out of here.'

'He will probably be dead anyway, before we get the story into print. But in the morning I have got to bring a photographer in, and a historian to identify him. And, yes, we'll get Mrs Morell out of the way. Least we can do.'

TWELVE

Saturday, June 10, 1967

There wasn't much to do during the night in the cramped Lotus except listen to the BBC World Service, and that had news almost exclusively about the Middle East. Fighting had stopped after six days, but only after Israel ignored Syria's acceptance of a UN ceasefire proposal and went on to bomb Damascus and advance to the Golan Heights, thus capturing more Arab territory than Israel itself had ever occupied. Total war casualties were estimated as at least one hundred thousand. The Egyptian Assembly had refused to accept President Nasser's resignation. The Soviet Union, reacting late to the conflict, was confidently expected to break off relations with Israel. The main news in the western world was that actor Spencer Tracy was dead. Katharine Hepburn had found his body.

There was no news from Ireland. But then, there never was.

When the sun hit the window Ritter turned to Merry. 'Right. I'm off to the airport. Nothing's gonna happen here. See you later.'

He collected his car from the Badgers yard, knocked on the Morell's front door, and opened his car door to assist Mrs Morell into the Rapier. As he put her suitcase in the boot her husband was knocking on the door of Mrs Brown's – Eva's – shop; good man, thought Ritter, he will need a bit of time to convince his patient of the necessity to go along with the interview and photograph. And with a song in his heart he drove off to Dublin, a familiar route by now. The car radio provided only background noise while he and Mrs Morell talked about the weather, then Ireland, then about wartime

Berlin. When the radio presenter announced Malcolm Arnold's Oscar-winning theme from *Bridge On The River Kwai*, Ritter turned up the volume.

'There are words to this, you know.' But she didn't know. And Ritter hummed along to the catchy marching tune forbearing, because Mrs Morell was a lady, to enlighten her by singing the words about the testicular count of the hierarchy of the Third Reich.

At the airport he collected the ticket Monica had ordered for Mrs Morell to go home to Munich, via London – the route he had taken only a couple of days earlier. Then he checked the departure and arrivals boards, and took her for a cup of tea. She did not notice a middle-aged man who appeared at the door with two miniature cameras; he took several dozen shots of the pair of them, clearly deep in conversation.

Later, when he escorted her to the departure hall, she offered him both cheeks to kiss, continental-style, and he noticed that she was crying. He hugged her. They had, he realised, become quite close over the last few days. He surprised himself that, apart from their first meeting, their friendship had developed over only a very few days. He would miss her almond cake.

He walked back to the buffet.

'Get the pictures?'

'Monty' Carlo tapped his camera bag. 'All in there, sunshine. Couple of rolls.'

Ritter turned to McKeown, who introduced him to Professor Blenkinsop, monocled media guru and professor of military history at Durham University. They all shook hands, then Ritter put his arm round his boss's shoulder and walked him away from the table.

'How's it going, Tex? Why have you dragged me into foreign territory?'

'You are not going to believe this, Bill. You are not going to believe it!'

'I always hate it when my reporters tell me I am not going to believe something,' the news editor told him. 'Because I always believe everything they say.'

'I got shot yesterday morning,' said Ritter. 'And I met Hitler yesterday afternoon.'

McKeown, spectacles in hand, was speechless for perhaps a minute.

Then he just said, 'Kinnell!'

Ritter expected the news editor to want to come back to the village with the team, but when he had briefed him fully – and he realised that there was not actually a lot of fact to impart from the otherwise extraordinary events of the previous day – McKeown announced that he would return to London.

He did agree that if Hitler was on the verge of death there was great value in holding the story for a day or so – if only to guarantee that the *Post*'s interview with him was conclusively the last one ever. But they had to get pictures of him, and then maybe they could hold the story only a day or so, and meanwhile, it was more than his job was worth if he did not pass on the news to the editor and Jake.

'But can they keep it to themselves, Bill… even for a day or so?'

'That is not the point, Tex. The point is that this story is bigger than you and me, and bigger even than them. I cannot not tell them. But I will go and see them in person. Kinnell! I had better ring them now, and get them both to meet me at the airport, I guess. Now, how much does Tom know?'

'He's up-to-date only as far as knowing we think Eva is alive.'

'So he doesn't know what he is baby-sitting?'

'I told you: I am not sharing this story with anybody, not even Tom.'

'OK. But you better brief Monty and Stan in the car on the way down. And you must tell Tom, the moment you get back. I can see that you don't want him to meet Hitler – tell him that's my decision, if you like. In any case, you will have a roomful in the bedroom with Monty and the prof. Now we have got to this stage, you'd better tell me where it's happening, and give me a number for the pub where you're staying, in case I need to reach you. Kinnell, Tex! You were right: I don't believe it. I mean... I know it's true. But I don't believe it!'

As they drove away from the airport, Professor Stanley Blenkinsop seemed to spend a lot of time polishing his monocle, then he told Ritter he didn't believe it, either. He had seen the death certificate, he said; apart from the fact that there had been a body, said Ritter, what did that prove? The Russians had identified the body, said Blenkinsop; well, said Ritter, they would, wouldn't they? It was a matter of history, Blenkinsop told him; history was bollocks, said Ritter.

'Well,' said the professor. 'We shall see. You know, I nearly met Hitler, once. And he settled down in the cramped space at the back of the Rapier, as relaxed as if he was on one of his frequent appearances on a TV chat show, and told the reporter and photographer about being deputed by Prime Minister Chamberlain to meet 'Herr Hitler.'

In 1938 he had been sent to Berlin, only to discover that Hitler had gone to Munich. He flew to Munich, by which time Hitler was in Nuremberg. He took a train to Nuremberg and Hitler was in Berlin. When he arrived in Berlin, Hitler was in Hamburg.

'So the meeting never actually took place and I returned home. Eventually, Mr Chamberlain went himself to Germany for the meeting – more than one meeting, as a matter of fact – the consequences of which the world is only too well aware. I often think that, if Herr Hitler had had the courtesy to keep his appointment with me, the whole course of world history might have been changed.'

Out of the corner of his eye Ritter watched the photographer's eyes roll heavenward.

'Quite,' said Monty Carlo, quietly.

Ritter turned the car radio on, to deter further conversation. He wondered how Morell had progressed, explaining to his famous patient – to his only patient – that he was about to be visited by a military historian, and to have his photograph taken for the first time since being photographed by Heinrich Hoffman. Monty Carlo, Ritter realised with a shock, was about to become world famous, too.

He flashed his lights at the Lotus as he drove into the village. Merry got out of his car and leaned against it, waiting while Ritter drove round to the back of the pub and parked. Then he walked back into the street and introduced Blenkinsop. Merry and Carlo greeted each other as if they had not seen each other for years, despite the fact that they would have been drinking together in the Glue Pot earlier in the week.

'It's been all quiet, here,' said Merry. 'The priest came round looking for you. Says he wants to see you, urgent. He's been a busy bee today, been in and out of Morell's house, in and out the shop. What you done – violated the village virgin? You told me you hadn't touched her. Anyway, Deirdre left the shop with him and he says again it's very urgent he sees you. Morell hasn't appeared all day, since he went over to the shop, first thing in the morning.'

Ritter looked across the road.

'How long has that tea towel been covering the clock in the shop window?'

He banged on the Morells' doorknocker. There was no reply. He banged again, and it seemed to echo inside. He tried the door: it was locked. And when he crossed the road to the shop the sign in the door said Closed, and meant it. Behind the door there was no sign of movement. The bedroom curtains were drawn, he noticed, but they usually were. He walked back across a deserted street to the car.

'Hang about,' he said. But when he went to the back door of the house, and then to the door behind the shop, he found them locked up and silent.

'Nobody's been in or out?'

'Not in the house,' said Merry, 'except for the priest.'

'What about the shop?'

'I don't know. A few customers, I suppose. I wasn't really watching. I bought some fags from your virgin early on. I think she probably locked up when she went out with the sky pilot. You can have the Camels back, any time you like.'

Ritter's stomach was starting to churn. He told Carlo and Blenkinsop to go and wait in the pub and then said, 'Tom, I have something to tell you...'

When Ritter finished the story, Merry told him: 'The only reason I am not putting you in hospital right now is that we have got to try and rescue something pretty quickly out of this total fucking fuck up. Get in the car, we'd better start at Deirdre's.'

Her brother-in-law opened the door. 'You'll be Mr Ritter, then. The friend of John Lennon's,' he said with a sneer. 'I'll get Deirdre, I suppose that's what you want.'

'Thank God you've come back,' she said. 'Have you seen Father Dennis? He wanted to see you as soon as you were back. I've got to talk to you.' She looked over her shoulder and saw her brother-in-law loitering. 'Not here. Come down the garden.' Ritter signalled to Merry and walked with Deirdre to a place where they could lean against the garden wall and talk confidentially.

'It's been awful, Charles, honest it has.'

Ritter grabbed her shoulders so hard that her breasts shook. 'What's been awful? What the fuck is going on. Tell me, for God's sake!' He was starting to feel sick.

'It's all right for me...' She sobbed. 'I'm only out of a job. But the others...'

'For God's SAKE!' Ritter was aware that he was shouting. He looked around, but there was nobody, apart from Merry, within earshot.

'Charles.' Deirdre started to weep. 'Father Dennis wanted to tell you. The Browns and Doctor Morell. They've all disappeared,'

'Where've they disappeared to? How could they go anywhere? Mr Brown was bedridden. They haven't got a car. Have they hired a car? They haven't got a phone. When was the last time you saw them? Tom's been outside the house all day.'

The Browns had vanished, she thought, some time during the night. Deirdre had opened up as usual about half past eight. The milkman came about nine thirty, but he brought his bill, so she shouted up the stairs for Mrs Brown and there was no answer. The milkman waited a few minutes in case she appeared but eventually he went off without his money. That was the first clue Deirdre had that something was amiss. The second was that the Morells' curtains, opposite, remained drawn across the windows. It was not absolutely unusual for Mrs Brown to remain upstairs at the start of the morning, but, Deirdre reckoned, she normally appeared by eleven at the latest.

'I shouted upstairs to see if everything was all right,' she said. 'But there was no reply. I go for my lunch at one, and she hadn't come down then, and there had been no sound at all, all morning, so I decided to go upstairs and look. I was terrified I might find the pair of them dead.'

The young girl had crept up the stairs as if noise might make a difference to whatever she might find. It was so dark she had to feel around for a light switch. The upper floor reminded her most of her grandparent's home. It was clean and tidy, but dark and old fashioned. The kitchen was spotless. Everything clearly put away after whatever was the couple's last meal. Deep in alien territory, she had knocked before trying the bedroom door. This room, too, had been empty. The bed perfectly made and the bed covers smoothed. The dressing table set – matching handmirror, hairbrush and comb – laid out as if part of a display.

'It looked more like someone was expected, than that it had just been left,' Deirdre told Ritter.

'Did you have a look in any of the cupboards or drawers?'

'No, of course not. Well, only the larder. I opened that because I didn't know whether it was another room. Everything there was lined up neatly, as well. Then I went downstairs because the shop doorbell rang. 'It was Father Dennis. He was a bit out of breath, and seemed a bit worried that I'd been upstairs. He said he knew the Browns had gone. He couldn't tell me where, but he'd tell me later. He asked me if I knew where you were and I said I thought you were not far away, but I didn't know where. He just said that I should keep the shop open for the time being until he told me, but not to order any goods but just keep selling what stock we had in. And he said that if I heard from you he wanted to see you straight away.'

'You've got the shop keys…'

'Yes of course. But you've got to see Father Dennis.'

'I'll go and see him, naturally. But first, let's have a look round the shop.'

Deirdre sat squashed in the back of the car, behind Merry, and they drove the short distance to the shop. She unlocked the front door and while the bell was still tinkling Merry and Ritter headed for the stairs.

'I'm not sure you should go up there. It might not be right.'

'Don't you worry, darling,' Merry said over his shoulder. 'You look after the place down there. We'll look after it up here. Back in a minute.'

Merry headed for the sitting room and started yanking drawers open while Ritter did the same in the bedroom. Neither knew what he was looking for. What would Adolf Hitler and Eva Braun have taken with them to Ireland when fleeing the Fatherland, that they might have abandoned in their flight from Ireland? Family snap shots? An Iron Cross? A spare Munich Agreement?

There were plenty of clothes shirts, pyjamas, nightdresses, underwear – all made in Ireland. But nothing reminiscent of wartime Berlin to be seen in either room.

Merry came to the bedroom door. 'What are we looking for? What should we expect to find, do you think?'

'I've no idea. It would be a start if there was anything. A clue to where they might have gone. Or anything at all, that was German, I suppose. Everything in here's Irish.'

Merry nodded in the direction of the sitting room. 'Everything in there is, too.'

'Keep looking. We'd better hurry up. If anybody catches us here we're in the shit.'

A few minutes later Merry called from the kitchen: 'Will an SS carving knife be any help?' Ritter rushed to his side. The knife, still sharp and shiny, was clearly inscribed with a German manufacturer's name.

'SS, you think?'

'It has that look about it.'

'Maybe it's a start. But it's not much, is it? It doesn't prove that the previous occupant was even German, nor a member of the SS himself, even if it is an SS knife. It certainly doesn't prove Hitler was here. Anybody could have brought that back from the war.'

'Or bought it in a junk shop on the Portobello Road.'

'Let's keep looking.'

'I'll keep looking. You go and see the priest.'

Father Dennis was in the presbytery garden when Ritter opened the high bronze gate.

'Charles, my boy! You were in Germany – how was it?'

'Full of krauts.'

'Of course,' he chuckled. 'It would be.'

'This place, on the other hand, appears to be totally devoid of them.'

The priest looked slightly shamefaced. 'We've got to have a talk about the couple you know as Mr and Mrs Brown. I gather that you have actually met Mr Brown.'

'Dennis. Do you know who the Browns are?'

'I'm afraid I do.'

'Then why in hell's name didn't you tell me instead of letting me fart about all that time asking you who was buried in which grave?'

'I'm sorry to say this, Charles. But the reason I didn't say anything about the Browns was that you didn't ask me. Not a word. All the questions you did ask me, I answered honestly and accurately, I think. I could hardly answer questions you didn't ask.'

'You could have helped me.'

'That's a pretty selfish view, you know. I could have helped you more, perhaps, but I also had to bear in mind the help I owed to members of my flock.'

'Your flock? The Morells?'

'Well, the Morells, yes. And Mrs Brown, of course.'

'Eva was a Catholic? I never knew that.' The priest shrugged his shoulders. 'Why should you know? Not everyone wears his religion on his sleeve.'

'Like a swastika, you mean? Or a yellow star? Deirdre said you've got something to tell me. Will you start by telling me where Morell and the Browns have disappeared to? Have you got them hidden away somewhere?'

'Not quite, Charles. Mrs Morell, well I gather you looked after her welfare. That was a kindness. She's had a quite awful life.'

'Don't bugger me about, Dennis! What about the others?'

The priest shook his head. 'That's where the problem, your problem, comes in, Charles. They're dead, I'm afraid. All dead.'

'They can't be,' protested Ritter. 'Three people can't just die like that. Not while I happen to be conveniently away in Dublin. You've got to be lying!'

'Normally, I suppose you'd be right. But you are ignoring the possibility of one factor. That they all died by choice.'

'Suicide, you mean?'

'All that has happened is that history has caught up with Adolf Hitler.'

'He was about to die anyway, Morell told me. Are you, a priest, saying you conspired with three suicides?'

'Conspired? Hardly. Remember, Hitler intended to die with Eva Braun in the bunker. He wanted to die in Berlin. And she with him. He prepared himself for it – according to the melodramatic history books he prepared for a Viking funeral. His mind was made up. Only Morell, and apparently Bormann, prevented this.'

'Hang on, Dennis. How long had you known that you had Adolf Hitler living in your parish?'

'Since before I came here. I was told about it in Rome. I was selected for the parish because of who lived here.'

'Why? What were your special attributes for the job.'

'Oh, I don't know. A knowledge of German – that certainly helped in the early days. Just that and a determination, I suppose, to prevent embarrassment to the Holy See. I understand that Doctor Morell told you about the Vatican involvement.'

'He told me about the Vatican helping him to get out, plus thousands of others. He didn't intend me to know anything about Hitler.'

'It's good that he was discreet about that. Italy had of course been both an ally and an enemy of Nazi Germany and at the end of the war became a natural sanctuary for some Nazis on the run. Rome especially, because of the presence there of Bishop Hudal – he had the same given name, coincidentally, Alois, as Hitler's father, did you know? – he was the Rector of the German Church there.

'Hudal and another priest, Eugenic Pacelli made a concordat with Hitler in 1933 that he would not persecute

Catholics nor oppose the Church of Rome. You haven't heard of Pacelli, I suppose?'

Ritter shook his head.

'No. But you'd have heard of Pius XII. He was Pope from 1939 to 1958, and he was the same man. It was he who sent me here. He had equivocated over the persecution of the Jews and he refused to condemn the Nazis, even when Hitler violated the concordat. The nearest he came was to ransom some Italian Jews with Church gold. Hudal, on the other hand, told the Germans that deporting Jews was bad for his country's – meaning Germany's – image and he did actually shelter some Jews in a monastery. Later, though, he gave shelter to Eichmann and Rauff, the Milan SS chief, and also to Reinhardt, the governor of Galicia... I wonder, now that you know that, will you be as discreet as Doctor Morell?'

'No, Dennis. I don't think so. I don't think I'll be even so discreet as to keep you out of it. There's nothing to stop me, now, identifying the village, either. That was the only deal I made with Morell, you know. That and getting his wife out of the way. Mrs Brown's shop now will become a tourist attraction like Braunau, or the Berchtesgarten, or the Berlin bunker. It will be depicted on Irish linen tea towels. You'll have a genuine Hitler shrine on your doorstep. Fame at last.'

'You can't do that – you'll ruin the place!'

'Tough titty, padre.' Merry, who had obviously been eavesdropping from behind the privet hedge, swung open the gate and walked in to the garden. 'All we want to do now is see the bodies, I suppose, and pull out of here. Where are they?'

Ritter introduced his colleague to the priest, and said: 'Yes; where are they?'

'Not where you can see them, I'm afraid. Doctor Morell is probably airborne by now, in a coffin, en route to Munich. In any case, I don't suppose that seeing his body would help anybody very much. Mr and Mrs Brown are – well, you can't see them.'

'Just a minute,' said Merry. 'How did you get these people out of their homes?'

'The Morell house, and the shop, too, they each have a back door. It hardly needed a magician to remove them.'

Merry studied his shoes. It had happened on his watch. But how could one man simultaneously watch two front doors and two back doors? 'OK, so how did they die?'

'The doctor I had sent for – he came from Dublin – found that Morell died of a heart attack. While I suppose it is remotely possible that this was the truth, my sincere belief is that he carried out the threat he made to me and committed suicide. I don't doubt that he had the technical ability to create a fatal heart attack. As for Mr and Mrs Brown, as I am now used to calling them, well… that was suicide by cyanide pill. That had always been the plan.'

'This doctor that you brought in,' said Merry. 'He was from the seminary I suppose?'

The priest nodded.

'I suppose you got your tame doctor to write out death certificates on them and avoid an inquest!'

'There was no need. Their death certificates were already written, signed, confirmed and published, twenty two years ago.'

'Still, the bodies must be somewhere,' said Merry. 'We need to see them.'

He looked at his watch. 'I'll show you what I can, but it will have to wait for just a while. Why don't we have a drink?'

He went inside and returned with three glasses and a bottle of Italian white wine.

As he pulled the cork, he said to Ritter: 'I said I didn't answer your questions because you hadn't asked any. That is true about Mr and Mrs Brown. But I did look up Mr Cully for you. I found some correspondence in the filing cabinet. When Mr Cully died it was established that his next of kin, a brother, same surname, was an officer on board a ship registered and owned in Panama, but currently steaming in the Indian Ocean. Mr Cully – the brother of the deceased – could hardly be expected to get back here in time for the funeral, but he did send a cheque, drawn on his employer's account, to pay for the costs of the funeral. Dr Morell told me that you had reached the conclusion that his body might have been Hitler's. If you had asked me, I could have told you that it wasn't. In fact I surely would have told you that it wasn't.'

'He had a lot of little scars or pits on his body, just as Hitler would have had, following the bomb attempt on his life.'

'Mr Cully was a roofer. Apparently he fell through a glass roof at some stage in his career. I suppose that might account for the wounds.'

The priest opened another bottle and when they had finished it he checked his watch again. He went indoors briefly and made a muffled phone call, then rejoined the reporters.

'Is your car outside? Let's go for a drive.' The priest went indoors for his jacket and for some reason unexplained, for a duffel bag, then sat in the front passenger's seat of the Rapier with the bag between his feet.

He directed Ritter to drive to the Lough and eventually to park the car near one of the jetties from which anglers occasionally fished, or yachtsmen set sail. They chose the one with no people about. The priest unfastened the duffel bag and produced two large white paper bags of the type that Deirdre used for wrapping boiled ham.

'My only crime,' he said, 'was to destroy dead bodies that the world did not believe existed. God will forgive me for that.'

'God might,' said Merry. 'But I won't. What do you mean, destroy?'

The priest looked again at his watch. 'The others will be here in a minute. Let's enjoy the view.' He sat with the bags on his lap as if he had brought sandwiches for a picnic lunch.

He looked again at his watch, and then at the road. Ritter followed his gaze and saw a red Audi hit the dirt road to the Lough.

Before the Audi reached them, a grey Triumph 2000 moved on to the road. Then an Austin Cambridge. Then a Vauxhall Viva. Then a man from Munich in a Pierre Cardin suit. Finally, a BMW motorbike.

None of them seemed pleased to see Ritter.

The priest told him: 'I left a message at the Badgers.' Then he addressed the assembled gathering:

'These,' he said 'are the earthly remains of Adolf Hitler and Eva Braun. You wanted to see them.'

He held up the paper bags and unrolled the folded tops to exhibit their white powdery contents.

'They have been cremated. These are their ashes.'

Then like a baseball pitcher he flung the paper packages, first one, then the other, far out into the Lough. The bags twisted and spiralled through the air, spewing trails of dust particles. When they hit the water they burst, spreading ash like a skein across the water. Then the skein, and the paper bags themselves, started slowly to sink.

For a moment, the motorcyclist looked as if he was about to follow the packet in to the Lough.

As it hit the water, the priest said: *'Requiescant in pace.'* And added, softly: 'Not, I suspect, that there's much chance of that.'

Of the assembled company, only Eli Bogart seemed content.

'Excuse me, reverend...' he said, 'While there are sufficient witnesses here to what has just happened, is there any proof – any proof at all – that the ashes are the ashes you describe?'

'Proof!' said the priest. 'Is it proof, now, that you're after? Well, the proof is the very fact that you are all here. Whatever proof it was that brought you all here individually, that is the proof you've got. There are some who would say that you should believe nothing unless you see it with your own eyes. I, of course, do not advocate that theory. But unless you believe what the world, generally, believes, about the demise of Adolf Hitler and his spouse, you are presumably ready to accept the alternative account, which involves his living beyond the spring of 1945. What I am telling you now is that if there were to be any truth in that account, then the life within that truth has now expired.'

He raised his eyebrows in request for further questions. Bill Bond had his hand in the air.

'You, sir,' said Father Dennis.

'Is he a friend of yours, this priest, or what?' Merry asked Ritter. 'What's he think he's running? – A fucking press conference?'

Ritter put his hand on Merry's arm to quieten him. 'Let's see what he's got to say.'

'While, of course, accepting everything that you say, Father,' said the man in the Pierre Cardin suit. 'I was not sure that cremation as we know it is widely available – if available at all – within the Republic of Ireland. Perhaps you can tell me where the cremation was carried out.'

'All I can tell you, sir, is that the cremation was carried out formally and within the requirements of health and legal requirements, although perhaps not strictly totally within the norm, at least, not in the Irish Republic. It was done not without risk, but it was done professionally.'

'He's got a kiln!' hissed Ritter to Merry. 'He cremated them in his own fucking kiln!'

'Did you do this yourself?' Bobby Sanchez was asking. 'Or was it done by the British government?'

'British government? The British government knew nothing about it. Although I suspect that Whitehall, like Washington and Langley, like Tel Aviv, and like Dzerzhinsky Square or Normannenstrasse, or wherever, will be satisfied with the result. Like Loch Ness's monster, the creature reared its head, but does not exist and will appear no more to worry us. The spectre is laid to rest. I cannot say we will hear no more of it, but we will know that it is dead, and out of the reach of mortal men.'

He looked at his watch. 'I trust there are no further questions, gentlemen?'

'I told you,' said Merry. 'He thinks it's a sodding press conference.'

'I have a question.' It was Bayer. 'You say those ashes were the remains of Hitler and Braun. I take it I can quote you on that?'

'To your superiors? Of course.'

'In my newspaper.'

'I'm sorry. I didn't realise that you were a journalist. What I said was off the record. It was information for you to possess, but not to print.'

'I'm not sure I can agree to that,' said Bayer. 'Where did Hitler die, and when?'

'As the world knows,' said the priest, 'Hitler committed suicide in Berlin in 1945. All we have here this afternoon is a little diversion.'

'Were those Hitler's ashes, or what?'

'If you play by my rules, mein Herr, they were Hitler's ashes. Hitler fulfilled his destiny and died by his own hand a few miles away from this very spot during the early part of today. If you reject my rules, then the package that you saw me throw was mere ash.'

'And what of Doctor Morell?'

'Dead too, I'm afraid. Of a heart attack.'

'A strange coincidence.'

'They do say that God works that way.'

His performance over, the priest turned to Ritter and Merry. 'Let's go back to the presbytery. I feel like a glass of wine.'

*

It had probably been inevitable, he told the two reporters, that, as soon as Morell had started talking to one person about the secret he had kept since the war, other outsiders would learn it. The Browns' paranoia about the Jews was both understandable and justly deserved, he said. 'And while Brown was certainly not entitled to any peace of mind he might just be alive today if you had not turned up on Morell's doorstep.'

'Christ, padre,' said Merry. 'We're not going to lose any sleep over the death of Hitler. He was a dead man anyway. All we've got to do is salvage a story.'

'And I'm just trying to fill you in on some of the details. After the amazing circumstances of your stumbling across Morell,' – he waved his glass in Ritter's direction – 'events seemed to take over from you. I don't know what you got up to but you attracted a veritable United Nations into this quiet backwater. Jews, Americans, Jewish Americans, Russians and Germans – and Britons. Not bad for a place where the village pub has only one guestroom.'

'I can't understand that at all. I know McKeown – that's our news editor – had this thing about his phone being tapped. But by the Yanks? And the Jews – you mean Israelis, do you?'

'I don't know. I don't suppose it makes much difference. Whatever, they turned up here and started asking questions. Even the English National Front sent somebody apparently, but they didn't get beyond the ferry. Your Irish friends saw to that. I must say you have friends in the most peculiar places, Charles. Nobody in the village, nobody except me, knew anything at all, but around here they don't easily answer outsiders' questions at the best of times. You will have seen that for yourself.'

'You're the awkward one,' said Ritter. 'You were the one who knew the answers, but avoided the questions.'

'You could hardly expect me to betray the sanctity of the confessional, could you?'

Merry asked him: 'Whose confession did you hear? Hitler was a catholic, wasn't he?'

'I was in fact referring to Doctor Morell. Hitler was indeed baptised a Catholic. He went to a monastery school and was actually a chorister in his youth. But I doubt I could've brought myself to hearing him confess. Nor, I suspect, for that matter, could any of the fathers through whose hands he passed in Italy. Not that he ever offered it. No: it was Morell's confidence I was respecting. But you did not ask me any direct questions about the Browns, nor about Hitler. If you had, then... I might well have lied to you, I suppose.'

'So, you were saying that nobody around here would tell anybody anything,' Ritter recapped. 'But they still felt sufficiently threatened to top themselves?'

'People were knocking at the door,' said Father Dennis. 'I mean, literally. You have to understand that they had been prepared for this eventuality – or, at least, had decided what steps they would be forced to take – for more than twenty years. Morell was the only one who needed to put his house in order, the Browns, naturally, had no affairs to organise.'

'There's the shop,' said Ritter.

'They were merely tenants. The shop, and all the furniture in it, belongs to the church. We merely look for a new tenant, which shouldn't be hard to find. Perhaps even Deirdre, if she wishes to spend the rest of her life here, which I don't think she does.'

'What outside affairs did the Morells have, then?' asked Ritter.

'Mainly, the safety of Mrs Morell. Then, I suppose, you.'

The priest refilled the glasses. 'I think it's reasonable to assume – don't you? – that if it wasn't for you, not only would the Browns be alive today, which may be of little consequence, and he may not have been very alive at that, but at least Mrs Brown would be, and so would Morell. I mean, even with Hitler's suicide there was no reason for Morell to die, was there?'

'What do you mean?' Ritter asked.

'That your presence made him the missing link. With Morell alive, there was a story. Without him, there was no proof that Hitler ever survived the bunker.'

'I hope, padre,' said Merry, 'that you're not suggesting that there's no story, after all that we've heard and seen today and all that he' – he nodded in Ritter's direction – 'all that he has got in his notebook.'

'I'm not a journalist, but I don't see what the story is,' said the priest.

'Shall I tell him?'

Ritter, who was now wondering himself what the story was, nodded, and Merry took a swill of his Italian wine and explained: 'First, contrary to what the entire world believed, Adolf and Eva did not top themselves and have their remains burned in the bunker.

'Second, they escaped, not only out of Berlin but also – and Chas here says the Brits fixed it, but there's also the involvement of your lot in Rome – all the way out of Europe and to the safety of Ireland whose so-called neutrality during the war was always in question, anyway.

'Thirdly, he actually lived in hiding for twenty-odd years over a corner shop—'

'And they had this system...' interrupted Ritter. 'Everybody is looking all the time at a clock, mostly without realising it... And the Morells spent all their time sitting in the window looking across the road. So when Hitler needed Morell – when he was feeling bad and needed another injection or whatever – Eva just put the tea towel over the face of the clock and Morell went running across the road to treat him.'

'Is that how they arranged it?' said Father Dennis. 'I never knew that, and that's the truth. Now, you're telling me things.'

Merry took another drink. 'Next,' he had stopped counting, 'he had his faithful wife, plus his doctor, with him. In fact the only one missing was his dog.' Again, the reporter paused for thought. 'And maybe Bormann. Jesus! I suppose there's no chance that he was here, as well?'

Father Dennis smiled and shook his head: 'No Bormann. You have my word on that.'

'And they live in peace until in an act which the public, the readers of the *Post*, anyway, would doubtless see as Christian, as a veritable Good Samaritan, Morell helps Charlie here to cure his headaches and he uncovers the whole dastardly plot.

'Next... and we must be on about point ten here, you tell us that the Jews – in whatever manifestation they appear – also discover the Führer and he tops himself.'

Merry raised his glass to the priest, and smiled. 'And you don't think that's a story...'

'Oh, I have no doubt that it's a story. A great story. You might tell it for years around your dinner table. What I don't think is that you can prove a single word of it.'

'Well, there's Morell's body, for a start.' said Ritter. 'He was supposed to be dead years ago, but you've told us that his body is probably en route, as we speak, back home to the land of kraut. That's the first piece of evidence.'

'But gentlemen, evidence of what? That Hitler lived in Ireland? And who cares about Morell? He was supposed to be dead, but he was alive, and now he's dead again. So what?'

'So, he was Hitler's doctor, and he's been looking after him since the war.'

'He was Hitler's doctor. The world knows that. The fact that Morell didn't die in Berlin proves nothing about Hitler.'

'There's Mrs Morell.'

'You can hound an old lady, if you like. But I think you should know that, when you talk about the Browns, for instance, Mrs Morell could hardly prove conclusively that Mr Brown was Adolf Hitler.'

'Of course she could,' said Merry and Ritter together.

'Prove it? I wouldn't think so. She could say it. She couldn't prove it.'

'Amazing claim of Hitler's doctor's widow – The Führer died in Ireland.' said Merry.

'But she's not going to make any such claim,' said the priest. 'Amazing or otherwise.'

'There's fingerprints,' said Merry. 'There must be fingerprints we could check and compare.'

'You'd think there would be. But actually there are none.'

'I'll tell you what there is, padre,' said Merry. 'There's one witness who is undeniable, whose evidence is unimpeachable. Who can tell the story from the beginning, in minute detail.'

'What do you mean?'

'What I mean is, there's you.'

'But I'd lie.'

'Not on oath, you wouldn't. Not on the Bible.'

'I've already thought about it.' He refilled the glasses. 'I can't think of the circumstances where I could be forced to swear on the Bible, but many years ago I came to the conclusion that, even if it meant that I was committed to eternal damnation, I'd lie. And I think, don't you, that in the circumstances the damnation might not be eternal? After all, there is always the consideration of the confessional.'

'Some sort of bloody priest, you are,' muttered Merry.

Father Dennis said: 'I do my best. But it is, of course, difficult to please all of the people all of the time. However, rendering unto Charles that which is Charles', and I might add, against my own better judgement, I have two messages for Charles here.

'The first is from Mrs Morell; she was aware of what her husband intended to do when she had gone away. She telephoned me from the airport to ask me whether it had been done, and said I should tell you that, in her words, "All that has happened is not Mr Ritter's fault." She is sorry, on behalf of her husband, that you were injured. I trust you are well on the way to recovery, now.'

'I can limp with the best of 'em.'

'The second is inside.' The priest rose from his garden chair and disappeared inside the presbytery.

'What do you reckon, Chas?'

'It's not the story I came for. But it's a story.'

'It's a bloody great story! First we had the British government freeing Hitler, then we've got the Roman Candles burning the bastard! Hang on a minute – Romans don't go in for burnings, do they? He'll roast in Hell, yet!'

The priest emerged with another bottle and a manila foolscap envelope. He applied a corkscrew to the bottle and turned to Merry: 'For a newspaperman, you are sadly out of date. It has been permitted for we Catholics to be cremated since His Holiness, in his wisdom, lifted the ban in July 1963 – and in fact priests have been permitted to perform cremations here... well, since you ask, since as long ago as September, last year.' Then he offered the envelope to Ritter: 'Apparently you'd asked for that. Keep it as a souvenir.'

'What is it?'

'I understand that it's Hitler's final testament. His explanation, and his message to the world.' Father Dennis shrugged and laughed softly as he spoke.

Merry got up and stood so that he could peer over Ritter's elbow. 'It's in German... What's it say?' Ritter scanned the two pages of spidery script.

'It's fantastic! The writing's atrocious, but it's incredible! Listen to this:'

I never wanted to go to war in 1939... I was provoked by international politicians who were either Jewish or working for Jewish interests... I made several offers of disarmament... I offered the French and British my hand, but they preferred war... you can't heap all the blame on me... The six years' war was a glorious and heroic manifestation of a nation's will to survive...

'Dennis – bless you! – you're a darling.' Ritter turned the page. 'It's not signed.'

'Mr Brown was too ill to hold a pen. He dictated it. The handwriting, I should tell you, is Morell's.'

'That's all you need, Charlie,' said Merry. 'You've got a deathbed confession. From Hitler.'

Ritter read on. 'It's amazing stuff, this.'

I will not fall into the hands of an enemy... I was betrayed by the officers of the German Army ... by Goering... by Himmler... Germany must now work to recover its lost territories, but above all uphold the racial laws in all their severity...

'Let's go now,' said Merry. 'Come on, Chas,' he half lifted Ritter, still translating, to his feet. 'Let's get out of here, while we're winning.'

'My own view about that document,' said Father Dennis, 'is similar to the rest of the picture. It proves that Morell was at some stage alive. But it proves nothing else.'

'It's Hitler's testament!' said Ritter.

'You and I know that, don't we? To anyone else, of course, it's what Dr Morell thought that Hitler's testament would have been. In years to come, it might be worth a few punts as a document written by Hitler's physician, if you could prove that he wrote it. But as proof that Hitler lived in Ireland – well, I'd doubt it.'

'Only one man could have written, or dictated this,' said Ritter, waving the flimsy lined paper in the air: 'Adolf Hitler.'

'You don't have to convince me, Charles,' said the priest. 'Only the world.'

*

Professor Stan Blenkinsop looked at the 'last testament', and appeared to experience difficulty in reading it. Ritter quickly gave him an encapsulated translation: 'It's Hitler saying what went wrong with the War, where he went wrong, what he wanted, who betrayed him, that he didn't want to go to war in the first place. It's amazing stuff!'

'To you, maybe. It might be slightly updated, but I've read it all before.'

'But it is updated.'

'Well, yes and no. The one I read – I have a copy on the wall of my study, actually – the one I have was actually signed by Hitler. This one is, well, it's only so much waste paper.'

'But Hitler dictated this, today, or last night. Here in Ireland!'

'Where does it say that? No, as you say, he dictated it. Perhaps. This isn't his handwriting. There is no signature. No date. It isn't witnessed. No; sorry, as far as the world is concerned, you could have written this.'

He rubbed the texture of the paper between his fingertips. 'It would help if even the paper was German, it wouldn't help a lot but, look' – he held it up to the light – 'E J Arnold and Son: it's even English notebook paper.'

'Well, bugger you!' said Ritter. 'Bugger Morell, bugger Hitler, bugger the priest, bugger the lot of you! I know I've got a story. Historians never know anything until it appears in the papers. I'm going to phone McKeown. We'll let him be the judge of this.'

Nevertheless, it was a subdued reporter who eventually stepped into the roadside telephone kiosk and interrupted his news editor's Saturday night.

'Bill,' said Ritter, with Merry at his elbow. 'We've got a really great Hitler story which we can file tomorrow morning and start running in Monday's paper.'

'Ritter,' said McKeown, 'I love you. What a pro you really are!'

'It's not absolutely the story we thought we were getting, I'm afraid. I mean, I've got quotes, and all that...'

'And pictures,' said McKeown, helpfully.

'Well, no. Not actually any snaps, but...'

'Why not, for Christ's sake?'

Well, look, Bill, it's still a good story, but the problem is, Hitler's dead.'

'Hitler's what...? What are you telling me here?'

'He's... well, he's dead. What's happened is that he and Eva committed suicide this morning. They took cyanide pills. And the bodies have been cremated. But it's still a good story, Bill!'

'You arsehole! You useless, snot-gobbling, arsehole! What do you mean, it's a good story?'

'Bill, it's Hitler. He's committed suicide. It's a great story!'

'A great story? Hitler has committed suicide and his body burned, a great story? Do you realise what you're saying? It WAS a great story, the first time we ran it, it was a great story! That was in 1945...! Now it's a heap of shit.'

'But Bill, at least I've got his last testament, his message to the world.'

'That could just rescue the situation. What's he say?'

'Oh, he didn't want to start a war, it wasn't his fault, he blames the German Army and Himmler, and that.'

'That's more like it, Chas, my son. You really had me worried, for a minute. Have you shown it to old Blenkinsop? He's the expert, after all. What does he say?'

'Well, Bill, actually, to be honest, he's not very keen. He says he's read most of this before. But what I've got, and Hitler dictated this for me personally, for the *Post* if you like, is how he sees it now, in the sixties, and looking back.'

'Great, kid. First class. Nobody's interested in that old fool's opinion. Who did Hitler dictate it to?'

'Morell. Hitler was lying in his bed. I asked him for his last message to the world through the *Post* and he dictated it for me, last night, literally as his last act on earth.'

'Kinnell! That's brilliant... Brilliant! At least Morell can corroborate it, then. Nobody will doubt the word of a doctor, not even Hitler's doctor. Especially Hitler's doctor. Did Morell certify his death?'

'Bill... Morell's dead as well.'

'For God's sake! Somebody must have given you this bloody testament! There must be some provenance.'

'Morell gave it to the village priest, to give to me...'

'That's great, Charlie. That'll do.'

'But the priest says he'll deny it.'

'Hang on.' Ritter could hear McKeown telling his teenage boys to keep their noise down. 'We've got Hitler's testament, signed, and we've got Hitler's body? Right? Ritter! I am right, aren't I?'

McKeown correctly interpreted the silence on the line, before Ritter started to fill him in with the facts. 'You haven't got Hitler's body, have you... because you've just told me it was cremated. I think you had better work out what it is you have got. Ring me in the office tomorrow morning, nine thirty,' he said, bitterly, and hung up.

'That's it, then,' said Merry as the two emerged into the street. 'That's everything pissed down the pan. I'm going to get legless in your pub. I suppose you're going to get your leg, or your good leg, across that girl from the shop. I don't blame you. I'm going to have a go at the landlady, I think.'

As they walked towards the pub Merry reached into the inside pocket of his jacket.

'Here,' he said. 'A souvenir for you.' He handed Ritter a postcard-sized photograph, clearly old, probably taken around the turn of the century. It showed a pale attractive woman in her forties with large bright eyes and high cheekbones. Her hair was almost brown and short and parted on the right. There was no mistaking whose mother she was.

In any case, he had seen something very similar in an oval frame at the foot of a stone plinth in Leonding.

'Where did you find this?'

'Would you believe under his pillow?'

*

Sunday, June 11, 1967

When he rang, Ritter found McKeown in no better mood.

'For your information, I've spoken to Jake, and Don. There's no argument, here. We're cutting our losses. The story is no further forward than before you started it. Nothing is new. Historically, nothing has happened. Pack your bags. Tell the team to come home. To report in the office tomorrow. Not you, I want you out of Ireland, and out of sight for a while, certainly for a week. I've spoken to Merry, he says he no longer wants to kill you... but I do. So best if you go – I don't know – go to Newcastle.'

'Bill, for God's sake. It's still a great story. The fact that he's dead doesn't alter anything.'

'That's the whole point. Exactly. Essentially. In a nutshell. Come on out of there. Nice try. Lousy failure. You should never have left the story. You've ballsed it up. You've also made me look a compete arsehole into the bargain, not that I suppose that matters very much. I'll see you in a week.'

'Bill, you can't just spike this. It's a great story, even what's left of it.'

'Spike it? There will be no copy to spike because you are not writing it! I'm telling you! No! That's my decision. And it's also the boss's.'

'Bill, if you don't want it, there's plenty of other papers who will.'

'Don't be a dickhead all your life. Somebody might pay you something for it, as a one-off, maybe the Yanks' shopping-mall scandal rags. But you know as well as I do – if you apply your tiny mind to it – that if this story ever sees the light of day, anywhere, ever, certainly in my lifetime, you'll never work in newspapers again.'

Before he put the handset down, McKeown added, as if as an afterthought: 'There is one thing, only one thing, that the world still wants to know about Hitler. And you've interviewed his doctor.'

'I know,' said Ritter. '…He had two balls.'

He could feel the migraines coming on again. And he was dying for a smoke.

*

Saturday, June 17, 1967

McKeown had rung Ritter twice during the week: on Tuesday, to tell him that the editor had been fired, nobody knew why, nobody ever did when editors were sacked, but the rumour was that it had followed a suggestion to the board from Downing Street, and Jake was acting editor; and on Wednesday, to invite him to his home on Saturday to celebrate the McKeown's wedding anniversary, and with instructions – not a request – to invite Sue, who readily agreed to attend.

The news editor's family was not normally keen on celebrating anniversaries, so the only diners were three couples: the McKeowns, the Morrises and the Ritters.

'I thought this would be an opportunity for you to meet the new editor,' McKeown told him. It had been as predictable as anything could be in Fleet Street.

'Oh, congratulations,' said Ritter, raising his glass.

'Thanks,' said Jake. '…And to meet my new deputy editor.'

'Congratulations, Bill. Couldn't happen to a nicer guy. So, who's taking over the news desk?' Ritter hoped they weren't thinking of offering the desk job to him, even if all, as it appeared, had been forgiven.

'I'm bringing Bradbury back from New York,' McKeown told him. 'Which creates a vacancy there. We thought you might like it. Not that we want you out of the way. Well, not just that we want you out of the way... In cash terms it's about the best-paid job on the paper. You could live in Manhattan, of course. But on the rates we are paying you could live out of town, even afford a place with a paddock. Don't make your mind up now. You can sleep on it.'

Sue Ritter took a packet of Rothmans from her handbag, lighted one, drew deeply on it and handed it to her husband.

'We'll sleep on it,' she said.

Postscript

On May 1 1945 in the occupied Norwegian port of Trondheim, Grand-Admiral Karl Doenitz, the officially appointed Deputy Führer, was ferried on board *Grille*, Hitler's equivalent of a 'royal' yacht that the naval chief was using as his command ship. There, from the foredeck, he broadcast the news that 'our Führer, Adolf Hitler, this afternoon at his command post in the Reich Chancellery, fighting till his last breath against Bolshevism, fell for Germany.'

However, after capture by Soviet forces entering Berlin, Hitler's valet Heinz Linge testified that on April 30 Hitler and Eva Braun had killed themselves in a suicide pact in the bunker and that he had carried his boss's uniformed corpse, wrapped in an army blanket (because he had been unable to find a Nazi flag) and laid it in a shallow grave, possibly a bomb crater, in the vegetable garden just outside the emergency exit. Then Eva's body, similarly wrapped, was laid beside it. Petrol – more than 200 litres – was brought in jerricans and poured over the corpses but for some extraordinary reason it at first failed to ignite. After making spills out of confidential reports he collected from the conference room, lighting them with his cigarette lighter, and throwing them at the bodies, flames finally erupted, creating a fierce funeral pyre in the shadow of an abandoned concrete mixer.

Also in Soviet captivity Otto Guensche, Hitler's SS adjutant, stated that he had started the fire himself with a lighted rag – a small but not insignificant difference – and that the bodies had been burned 'until nothing remained', then that the ashes, 'which crumbled at a touch', were taken away.

There were no witnesses to the actual suicides of either of the deceased.

On May 2 President Harry S Truman told reporters that he had 'official information' that Hitler was dead. But neither he nor anyone else in Washington could offer any substance for the claim.

Professor Hugo Blaschke, Hitler's dentist, escaped capture but his secretary, Fraulein Kathe Heusermann, was arrested by the Russians in early May and was shown dental work (dentures and other fittings) from which she said she was able to identify her employer's handiwork as that performed on Hitler in the laboratory of the Chancellery the previous November.

One week later Soviet Security Police denied reports from Hitler's inner circle that Hitler had shot himself, taken poison or been cremated – or even that he had died in any way.

Harry Mengerhausen, a member of Hitler's bodyguard, claimed to have personally dug a three-feet-deep grave and buried the charred remains of Hitler and Eva in the garden. After being captured by the Russians at the end of May 1945, he says, he was shown three bodies that he identified as those of Hitler, Goebbels and Frau Goebbels. He said that the fire had not destroyed Hitler's body, nor even made it unrecognisable. Mengerhausen is the only person who has publicly claimed to have seen Hitler's body after April 30.

At a meeting in the Kremlin on May 26 Soviet leader Josef Stalin told US diplomats that Hitler had escaped and was 'in hiding in the West'.

On June 9 Soviet commander Marshal Georgi Zhukov told a press conference (his first in Berlin): 'We have not identified the body of Hitler. I can say nothing definite about his fate. He could have flown away from Berlin at the very last moment – the state of the runway would have allowed him to do so.' On the same date the Soviet military commander of Berlin said: 'We have found several bodies that might be Hitler's but we cannot state that he is dead. My opinion is that he has gone into hiding and is somewhere in Europe.'

That month at the Hotel Raphael in Paris General Dwight D Eisenhower, the supreme allied commander, told a press conference that he doubted reports that Hitler was dead.

Over lunch with other allied leaders at the Potsdam Conference on July 17 Stalin insisted that Hitler was still alive and 'probably' living in Spain or South America.

In August an American lawyer reported to the FBI that Hitler was living under an alias in Innsbruck 'with his personal physician'. Other reported 'sightings' of the ex-Führer included the Swiss Alps, Evian and Grenoble in southeast France, Lake Garda in northern Italy and 'a ship off the Irish coast'.

In September the Russian newspaper *Isvestia* reported that Hitler and Eva had 'been given sanctuary in the British zone of occupation'.

In October 1945 in Utrecht, Holland, Eisenhower, quoted in *The Times* (London), told journalists that although at one stage he had believed Hitler to be dead, 'there is now reason to believe that he is alive'. He also said that the Russian allies had assured him 'they had been unable to unearth any tangible evidence of his death'.

On November 1 Major Hugh Trevor-Roper (later Lord Dacre), an Oxford history don assigned by British Intelligence to investigate reports of the death of Hitler – and also to put an end to Russian allegations that there had been any British complicity in his escape – told a press conference that, mainly based on evidence of people who had been told about the death by such 'eye-witnesses' as Linge and Guensche, he believed the Hitler-Braun suicide pact story. Asked whether he was aware of the Russian view, he admitted that the Soviet authorities 'were inclined towards the view that Hitler was still alive'.

In 1952 Eisenhower, now US president, stated: 'We have been unable to unearth one tangible bit of evidence of Hitler's death. Many people believe he escaped from Berlin.'

In 1955 Linge told the *News of the World* in a series of interviews that – *although he had not personally witnessed it* – he had been told that the bodies had been burned and then buried in a bomb crater...

In 1969 West German police arrested an 80-year-old man they believed to be Adolf Hitler, but who was eventually able to prove incontrovertibly that he was (and always had been) called Albert Pankla, a retired miner.

In 1970 Russia announced that Hitler's remains had been cremated and the ashes scattered in the River Ehle near the village of Biederitz, East Germany. Originally discovered on May 4, 1945, they had most recently (February 1946) been interred in Klausernerstrasse, Magdeberg, about 70 miles from Berlin, beneath a garage behind the local headquarters of the Soviet 3rd Army counter-intelligence unit that had originally discovered them. They had been dug up and reburied several times as the unit moved around the country during 1945 and were finally completely destroyed when the building was being handed over to the East German authorities.

In 1993 Moscow announced that it had fragments of Adolf Hitler's skull 'found in a hole where his body had been buried'.

In April 2000, a four-inch bone fragment with what appeared to be a bullet hole and was said to be a piece of Adolf Hitler's skull was put on display under thick glass in the National Archives in Moscow as part of a presentation entitled *The Agony Of The Third Reich*. It was now claimed that the charred remains of Adolf Hitler and Eva Braun were discovered by the Red Army during its invasion of Berlin but that part of Hitler's skull had been missing. In July 1946, the Russians had conducted a search of the area around the Berlin bunker and discovered fragments of a skull with a bullet hole in it. The bodies of Hitler and Eva were now said to have been kept in Moscow while the skull fragments – this is long before the vogue for DNA testing – had been retained by the KGB. In 1970, it was stated, the corpses were finally destroyed on orders from Leonid Brezhnev and the skull fragment retained for posterity. Associated Press quoted an official from the State Archive as saying that there was no documentation to prove that the skull was Hitler's.

The exhibition included a 1945 photograph, taken at considerable distance, of a partly charred body (said to be monorchid) in a wooden shell crate. The face and head of the body in the photograph, although not obviously identifiable as Hitler's, appeared to be intact.

The end?